D1450305

Stepping Forward

Encouragement for your walk with Christ

By Scott Shaw

Foreword

Barnabas is presented to us as the "son of encouragement" (Acts 4:36) with the express purpose of providing an example. He undergirded the Apostles and the Jerusalem Church with his financial gift, and he specifically singled out Christians that needed encouragement--like John Mark in Acts 15. It is in this context that Scott Shaw began writing a blog during the COVID-19 pandemic, the title of which is Encouraging Everyone. Scott believes deeply in the power of encouragement among Christians, and he has been a profound example of Christian encouragement to me.

In Hebrews 3:13 we receive what could be called the thesis behind this book: encourage one another daily. Each devotional reading is designed to take a quick look at a Bible text and will lay out key applications. We also see in our Hebrews passage the reason encouragement is so important: so that Christians don't fall prey to sin and its deceit. In this light, encouragement from other believers is essential to our daily lives if we want to please God. There are two ideas you can hold on to while you read this book: be encouraged, and be an encouragement.

As you read this book, be encouraged! First, be encouraged by the scriptures. Each passage included was designed by God to be the "bread" of the Christian life. Second, be encouraged by the existence of people like Scott. There are Christians around the world that desire to live the Bible out in their thoughts and actions. Scott is one of these men, and this book exists to prove that you are not alone in this walk. Third, be encouraged by your brother's experiences. Scott's life has been full of input from strong believers and God's provision; there is much to glean from him.

After you read this book, be an encouragement! If you benefit from this work, it is because of another person's constant resolve to encourage others. Equip yourself with the same resolve.

Finally, I pray that this book would accomplish the work of Barnabas: to undergird the Church and her members.

Andrew Bryant
Jefferson City, MO

Acknowledgements

I would like to thank my wife, Grace Shaw, for loving me and being such an excellent wife and mother. I love you very much. I am grateful for our three precious children; we have so many adventures ahead of us.

I am thankful for my parents, Gene & Annie Shaw. I love all the fun memories we have.

I would also like to thank Andrew Bryant, Dawn Jenkins, and Carolyn Patterson for editing this book. A big "thanks" goes out to Larry & Lynda Jones for encouraging me to continue to write during the pandemic of 2020. Luke Jones also deserves a "shout out" for designing the excellent cover.

I am grateful for my church family at Living Hope Church in Jefferson City, Missouri. The love that is shared within this local body of believers is very special to me.

Note: Some names in this book have been changed to protect people's privacy.

TRAIL MAP

A Listing of Each Installment

Chapter 1:
Walk by Faith!

(7 Devotional Readings)

Higher Ground

Have you ever wondered why some people are able to rise above the storms of life and other folks are more easily brought down by difficult circumstances?

A solid upbringing sets some people up a little better than others for handling challenges, but the *big question is...* where do you find your support? Many people would answer that they find their support from their family. It is no doubt a very good thing to have a great support system of family and friends, but *do you lean on God to support you and lift you up?*

We should all be thankful that God uses people in our lives to encourage us and build us up, but His arms are wide open for you to come directly to Him. <u>We primarily do this through prayer and through His Word</u>. In the good times and the bad times, He is willing and waiting for us to come to Him to give us life and peace.

Let's look at Psalm 61 to see what God's Word says about how He lifts us up. This psalm can help us discover what life could be like if we rely on God every day.

As we rely on Him, we will experience...

1. Security from God

In Psalm 61:1-2 David says, *"Hear my cry, O God; listen to my prayer. From the ends of the earth I call to you, I call as my heart grows faint; lead me to the rock that is higher than I."*

Charles Ryrie helped me see the concept of the rock being a place of security when he explained this psalm, "Disheartened, David prays for security."[1] You can call out to God no matter your situation. He is a *good God* who is for us and not against us, and He will provide *security* in your life as you lean on Him.

2. Strength from God

"For you have been my refuge, a strong tower against the foe." (Psalm 61:3)

A simple yet profound truth is shown here: *God provides strength to His people.* The tower is a place of protection and safety, and when the Israelites were in a battle, they wanted a place of strength that was fortified and hard to attack. That is the picture that David uses to describe God. What powerful imagery!

The Lord lifts us up to a higher place (i.e. "a tower") and we are able to rise above the storms of life. Rising above life's difficulties is absolutely vital, and it provides a transition to our next point... God likens himself to a mother bird in Psalm 61 and Deuteronomy 32:11. He teaches us to fly and He also provides us with shelter...

3. Shelter from God

"I long to dwell in your tent forever and take refuge in the shelter of your wings." (Psalm 61:4)

Our mighty Lord is like a strong mother eagle that protects its baby birds under the shelter of its wings. His sheltering presence is where we sleep in peace each night and where we draw close to His love. He provides a safe tent for us, but it is also a place of preparation. The mother eagle prepares the baby eagles to eventually fly themselves over the torrents that life brings. Deuteronomy 32:11 declares, "Like an eagle that stirs up its nest and hovers over its young, that spreads its wings to catch them and carries them aloft." God will provide shelter for us in the nest, but He wants to launch us out to make a difference in the world.

He is the shelter that protects us from the calamity of this world; our job is simply to continue to come to God, our Great Shelter.

So there you have it! God is our refuge! Psalm 61 is a great Psalm that reminds us to go "to the rock that is higher than I." God will lead us to the rock. The rock of His Son. First Peter 2:4 uses the word **living stone** to describe Christ, "And coming to Him as to a living stone which... is precious in the sight of God."

Through His Spirit, we have Jesus by our side every day. He is the Rock of Ages who gives us security, strength, and shelter!

---

1. *Ryrie, Charles C. Ryrie Study Bible: New American Standard Bible, 1995 Update.* Chicago: Moody Press, 1995. Print.

Open Arms

Through the years, I have heard many interpretations of the parable of the prodigal son. I've even heard the parable go by different titles; here are a few that I've heard: 1) the parable of the lost son, 2) the parable of the two lost sons, 3) the parable of the merciful father. Many people have tried to get to the bottom of what was really being communicated by Jesus in Luke 15, but it often seems like people misunderstand this parable.

One thing we do know about the theme of this parable is that it is actually the third in a series of three parables in Luke 15. All three of these stories are about rejoicing when lost things are found (i.e. lost sheep, lost coin, lost son). The Pharisees were the target audience of these parables.

Look at Luke 15:1-2. "*Now the tax collectors and sinners were all gathering around to hear Jesus. But the Pharisees and the teachers of the law muttered, 'This man welcomes sinners and eats with them.'*"

Jesus wants to show the compassionate love of God that extends to all people. And He knows it will rub the Pharisees the wrong way when they see that they are the older brother in the parable of the prodigal son. They can't handle the father lavishing merciful grace onto the younger son who has been wildly disobedient (and is coming home with his tail between his legs).

Let's look at the younger son's journey toward home, and then we'll proceed to the older son.

Luke 15:20 says, "*So he [the younger son] got up and went to his father. But while he was still a long way off, his father saw him and was filled with compassion for him; he ran to his son, threw his arms around him and kissed him.*"

The younger son did not expect such a wonderful reception from his father, but that is what he received because he had a gracious father (and we have a gracious Heavenly Father). The older son was filled with jealousy for his brother and disdain for his father.

Luke 15:28a states, "*The older brother became angry and refused to go in [to the celebration for the younger son's return].*"

Can you believe how this sounded to the Pharisees' ears when they heard this parable? They were obviously a picture of the older brother, and the parable clearly depicts them as a salty people who lack grace. This parable masterfully shows the Pharisees' dilemma with law and grace. They were essentially 100% about the law and 0% about grace. But the beautiful thing about Jesus is that He fulfilled the law and He freely offers us His grace.

God's grace is immeasurable at all times. The act of the father receiving the repentant younger son is a beautiful picture of salvation. The son came with absolutely nothing, depending completely on the mercy and grace of his father. And just like our perfect Father, the father in the parable had **open arms**.

God's grace is bountifully shown in Christ and it is also shown in the third Person of the Trinity. God gives us the Holy Spirit. The Holy Spirit graciously works in our life at our salvation and He continues His work in our life for our sanctification. What a great God He is!

And one more thing about law and grace. The Holy Spirit helps us obey the commandments of God (His law). And even when we make mistakes [sin] God's grace abounds! God's Spirit helps us grow in maturity and transforms our life so that we become increasingly more like His Son. Amen!

The Pharisees just didn't want to accept this foundational truth about our God: **He is a God of grace.**

The more I've thought about it, I think the _parable of the merciful father_ is an appropriate title of this story of grace that Jesus told. The three main characters are important, but the father is the central figure because of his great love. Let's see what we can learn from each character in this well-known (yet often misunderstood) parable.

1. the younger son... We trust the Lord completely and come to Him in repentance and faith. We rejoice in our salvation and we celebrate a continual feast with our Father and fellow believers.

2. the older son... We avoid being judgmental and we avoid putting up barriers for people who are coming into the Father's family. We need to rejoice when someone comes in. Receive them warmly.

3. the father... We need to stand in awe of God's amazing mercy and grace. We need to glorify Him for being an awesome Father and continually give Him thanks.

Ready for a Breakthrough

Today, we will look at a powerful passage in the Gospel of Luke about a crippled woman being healed by Jesus. These four verses of Scripture show us that Jesus grants people true rest, freedom, and joy.

<u>Luke 13:10-13</u>

10 On a Sabbath Jesus was teaching in one of the synagogues,

11 and a woman was there who had been crippled by a spirit for eighteen years. She was bent over and could not straighten up at all.

12 When Jesus saw her, he called her forward and said to her, "Woman, you are set free from your infirmity."

13 Then he put his hands on her, and immediately she straightened up and praised God.

In this passage we see that Jesus was teaching in a synagogue on a Sabbath, the Jewish day of rest. There was a woman with a disability who was in attendance. She came to the synagogue on the day of rest even though her body, most likely, rarely felt at rest. After her encounter with Jesus, this woman would ultimately not only receive rest for her body, *she would receive rest for her soul*.

The crippled woman is called by the sinless Son of God to come up to the front of the synagogue. So she comes shuffling up to Him and He says to her, "Woman, you are freed from your disability."

Maybe you've been dealing with something in your life and you need to hear the voice of the Lord (just like the woman heard the voice of Jesus). You need to hear Him say to you, "I love you. You are mine. I'm going to take care of you."

In Matthew 11:28-30, Jesus speaks comforting words like these for any who would come to Him. He says, "Come to me, all you who are weary and burdened, and I will give you rest. Take my yoke upon you and learn from me, for I am gentle and humble in heart, and you will find rest for your souls. For my yoke is easy and my burden is light."

So, back to Luke 13:10-13... Jesus speaks to the woman that she is healed, and then in verse 13 an important *point of contact* takes place;

Jesus touches her. This is no small thing! The text says that "He laid His hands upon her and immediately she straightened up and praised God."

With the touch of Jesus, things change! It says that she straightened up *immediately*, so the power of God was being shown to all who were in attendance at the temple. She just starts praising God.

She releases her praise because she knew she was free. For almost two decades she had been saddled with this disability, and now she wasn't shackled anymore.

Just like the woman experienced God's healing presence, the Lord wants us to *come near to Him* and experience His healing touch.

I believe God wants all of us to stand tall and rejoice (like the woman did at the end of the passage), even as we wait for our breakthrough. We can rejoice because we have the risen Christ in our lives. We have the victory! We know that God provides in all circumstances.

It is important to note that it's not just physical healing that He wants to provide. We see the woman healed of her disability in this passage and we may think this passage is all about physical healing. However, the main message is that God wants to provide spiritual healing in our lives and, ultimately, long-term spiritual health.

Earlier in this post I said that this passage shows us that Jesus offers three important things. He provided these three things for the crippled woman and He provides these three things for us, too. So, here are the three keystones that Jesus provides for our full deliverance and spiritual vibrancy.

1. He brings true rest.

2. He brings freedom.

3. He brings joy.

Planting Seeds

I have met many people in life who have told me stories about their friends or relatives who have gotten on the wrong path and strayed away from God. They often share how they've become disheartened and concerned that their *loved one* won't come back to the fold. Whether it's a sibling, a spouse, a long-lost friend, or even an *extended family member*, the pain is real for the person waiting and praying for their friend to "come home."

As I've heard these people's stories and conversed with them, I recall the importance of **planting seeds.** Rarely do these wanderers come home right away, but many of them come home eventually. Therefore, the concept of planting seeds is very important because each seed of the gospel that is planted in love is one more positive influence that the wanderer is experiencing.

When I step back and think about it, the seed-planting we do with our loved ones who have strayed is virtually the same seed-planting we do with all people who have not yet confessed Christ.

There is a parable that the Lord Jesus told about *the sower and the four soils.* This parable is actually the *chief parable* that all the other parables build on. Jesus had several different types of people that were represented in the story.

Matthew 13:3 says, "Then He told them many things in parables, saying: "A farmer went out to sow his seed."

One key thing that I want to point out is this parable probably sounded different to the disciples than it did to anyone else listening to it. If you were simply a person in the crowd (and not a disciple) that definitely affected the way you heard the parable.

A person in the crowd may have first looked at it from an agrarian point of view, thinking about actual seeds and crops and different kinds of soil. And the application for those folks (if they have ears to hear) is that they need to allow the Word of God to work in their life and accept the gospel. In this way, they would be good soil and reap a great spiritual harvest.

For the disciples, they most likely heard this parable as a story that Jesus told them about evangelism. They would hear and understand "the path" (v.4), the "rocky places" (v. 5), and the "thorns" (v. 7) as people who would ultimately reject their message when Jesus sent them out to go evangelize. Obviously, the "good soil" (v. 8) is people who would accept the message and the large harvest was to show **the power of the Word of God being sown**.

That last phrase is important: *the seed is the Word of God.* When we plant seeds in people's lives, we need to be planting Biblical truth. Even sharing a verse or telling them a short story from the Bible can go a long way. They may not respond in a big way right away, but it is a seed that has been planted and God uses those seeds as He works in their life.

So, how were the disciples supposed to apply this parable? What is the application for us?

1. Recognize the power of God's Word.

2. Share the Word generously with many people.

3. Don't become discouraged when people don't respond affirmatively.

We would save ourselves a lot of heartache if we just regarded ourselves as sowers of seed and we simply trusted God with the outcome. Our job is to *keep spreading seed.* We could turn that into our mantra, "just keep spreading seed."

I hope that you will continue to spread seed in the coming weeks and months, and perhaps you'll feel emboldened to toss out even more seed that you have in the past.

A great harvest is on the way. I know we don't see it yet, but I can guarantee you that we will see a harvest of "a hundred, sixty, or thirty times what was sown." (v. 8) So, leave the results up to God, and just keep spreading seed.

Faith over Fear (Part 1)

As we go through life there are times when it feels like a calm day at the beach, but other times we feel the strong winds of uncertainty and it causes us to become afraid.

As Christians, we know that we should strive to have our lives consistently marked by faith and not fear, but what do we do when the winds of this life become incredibly strong? Where do we turn when we feel overwhelmed by fear?

The disciples had a life-changing experience in a boat when Jesus came to them, walking on the water. The Gospel of Matthew is where we will turn to today to read this account.

We'll pick up the story with the disciples in the boat. They were already experiencing strong winds. Let's look at Matthew 14:24.

And the boat was already a considerable distance from land, buffeted by the waves because the wind was against it.

So, they are in a difficult situation. They have come to the end of their resources and they are in a predicament and in need of rescue.

Now, we see Jesus coming to their aid.

Shortly before dawn Jesus went out to them, walking on the lake. When the disciples saw him walking on the lake, they were terrified. "It's a ghost," they said, and cried out in fear. But Jesus immediately said to them: "Take courage! It is I. Don't be afraid." (Matthew 14:25-27)

When Jesus says the phrase "It is I" you may think that He is saying a normal statement signifying that it really is Him on the water. However, when Jesus speaks out "It is I" He is actually making a powerful statement because He is referencing His Deity. In the Old Testament, God revealed Himself to Moses as "I AM." In this masterful statement of "It is I" by Jesus to the disciples out on the water, Jesus is essentially saying that He is Lord over creation.

In this section of Matthew, Jesus shows the disciples that He has authority and power over all things, including the winds, provision of food resources, and even the demonic realm. He feeds the five thousand with just five loaves and two fish. This is a massively important event because Jesus shows His all-sufficient power to multiply resources, feeding all the people from virtually nothing and there was food left over.

In Matthew 15, we see Jesus heal the daughter of a Canaanite woman who was oppressed by a demon.

The point of all these miraculous events by Jesus is not just to show His power over all things, but it is to *increase the faith* of the disciples and anyone else who encountered Him.

The disciples were gaining a greater awareness of who Jesus was. Their faith was increasing and Jesus was guiding them to exercise faith instead of fear.

The words are powerful and should not be overlooked. Jesus declared to the fear-filled disciples, "Take courage! It is I. Don't be afraid."

In some sense, He says those words to each of us today. Let us hear the voice of Jesus saying to us...

Take courage! (He is with us.)

It is I. (Trust Him! He is over all things.)

Don't be afraid. (Give your fears over to Him.)

May your faith increase!

As we go through these next weeks and months, let's all choose to exercise **faith over fear**.

__Faith over Fear (Part 2)__

In many parts of the Midwest there are corn mazes that pop up during the fall season. Many families and groups are able to take advantage of this seasonal staple, and they make fun memories as they try to navigate through the labyrinth of cornstalks.

If you try one of these mazes on an autumn afternoon, it can be a great way to enjoy some sunshine and temperate weather. However, if you try to conquer the corn maze at dusk you may find yourself lost as you are running out of daylight. Some families and teen groups intentionally go at night to increase the challenge. They will usually bring several flashlights along, but without the light of the sun the difficulty level is much higher.

In some of these Midwest corn mazes, they will add some scary elements to the maze after dark in order to make it more exciting for the evening participants. These "haunted" corn mazes are filled with surprises, thrills, and fear-filled moments. While fear is understood to be part of the event for a corn maze, in our daily lives it is best for us to exercise faith over fear as we give our anxieties over to God (See 1 Peter 5:7). The apostle Peter had a thrilling, yet fearful, event take place in his life on a lake as he stepped out of a boat. Let's read about it beginning in Matthew 14:28.

28 "Lord, if it's you," Peter replied, "tell me to come to you on the water." 29 "Come," He said. Then Peter got down out of the boat, walked on the water and came toward Jesus.

Wow! Peter is having an experience of a lifetime! He is walking on top of water....something humanly impossible! He is trusting Jesus and faithfully moving toward His master; what could be better?!

It really is amazing when you think about it. Peter is a positive example in this moment. He took a wonderfully bold step by getting out of the boat and stepping onto the water. He obeyed the call of Jesus and he is literally experiencing the power of God. What a rush!

But then the story takes a turn...

30 But when he saw the wind, he was afraid and, beginning to sink, cried out, "Lord, save me!" 31 Immediately Jesus reached out his hand and caught him. "You of little faith," he said, "why did you doubt?"

Peter looked at his circumstances instead of focusing on Christ, and he begins to sink. That is a very instructive picture for us. If we look at our circumstances instead of focusing on Christ, we will begin to sink. Thankfully, when we call out to the Lord in our *sinking situation* He lovingly reaches out His hand (just like He did for Peter) and rescues us. Jesus gives an admonishment to Peter for doubting and only having "little faith."

32 And when they climbed into the boat, the wind died down.

Did you see it? After they climbed into the boat, the wind died down and this is actually a sign <u>that Jesus has power over creation</u>. Even the winds and the waves have to submit to Christ.

The proper response to being in the presence of Jesus and witnessing a marvelous act of God **is simply to worship.**

33 Then those who were in the boat worshiped Him, saying, "Truly you are the Son of God."

This last verse is very important because the disciples have now come to a deeper understanding of who Jesus is. Jesus wanted them to know that He is the **Son of God** so He showed them that He had the authority and power of God.

So, what are some *key takeaways* from this passage today? We have established that we need to exercise faith over fear, but what are the main lessons that we are to heed?

<u>**S.T.E.P.**</u>

Set your eyes on Jesus

Take a step out of the boat (which is your usual place of comfort)

Encounter Jesus in the midst of your storm

Proclaim that He is the Son of God

Full Circle

At the time of this writing, my wife (Gracie) and I have been married for nine years. We were married on a beautiful sunny day in central Wisconsin on August 27, 2011. It was a great ceremony and I have re-watched it several times on our "Wedding DVD." My wife and I will always fondly remember that day, and the passage that was printed on our wedding bulletin was Ephesians 5:1-2.

I was reading in Ephesians chapter 5 today, and I saw the word '*walk*' jump off the page. "Walk" showed up in verses 2, 8, and 15. It was as if the text was screaming [loud and clear] that this is the key word of this entire passage... and I have read this passage a hundred times and hadn't noticed it!

So, let's look at how the word *WALK* shows up in Ephesians 5:1-16.

1. Walk in love.

"*Follow God's example, therefore, as dearly loved children and walk in the way of love, just as Christ loved us and gave himself up for us...*" - Eph. 5:1-2a

2. Walk as children of light.

"*For you were once darkness, but now you are light in the Lord. Live as children of light.*" -Eph. 5:8

3. Walk wisely.

"Be very careful, then, how you live—not as unwise but as wise, making the most of every opportunity, because the days are evil." -Eph. 5:15-16

The Greek word for 'walk' is *peripateo* and it means to walk in a full circle. HELPS Word-studies says that this word means "to walk around or in a complete circuit (going 'full circle')."[1] Strong's Concordance says that peripateo not only means *walk*, but it also means *the way you conduct your life.*[2]

The way that we conduct our lives as believers should bring glory to God. These verses in Ephesians show us that we should be living a life of love and we should be walking in uprightness and wisdom.

So here is what I am picking up from this passage. In regards to *walking*, we are called to do the following three things: 1) walk the full circle of love, 2) walk the full circle as children of light, and 3) walk the full circle of wisdom.

When I envision us walking these three circles as believers, I think of Jesus being in the center of the circle and God's light shining down on us so we can see where we are stepping. We are called to walk in the power of the Holy Spirit as we are continually filled with Him (Eph 5:18).

Here is my question for you today... Going forward, are you ready and committed to walk full circle with Christ on a daily basis?

Every day we take a step. We need to take that daily step forward on the path He has for us. Not a step backwards or a step to the left or to the right. We need to listen to His voice through His Word. Isaiah 30:21a says, "And your ears shall hear a word behind you, saying, 'This is the way, walk in it.'"

Thankfully, the three circles we talked about today (love, light, and wisdom) are really ONE circle. They are the circle of **Jesus Christ**. He is our love, our light, and our wisdom. In order to walk this journey of *love* and *wisdom*, we need the *light* of **His Word**.

Remember the words of Psalm 119:105, "Your word is a lamp to my feet and a light to my path." God uses His Word to illuminate our pathway and to help us keep our eyes on Jesus. Stand tall! And step forward with confidence and strength.

So, are you ready to go *full circle*?

Enjoy your walk today!

---

1. *HELPS Word-studies*. Helps Ministries, Inc. 2011. https://biblehub.com/greek/4043.htm

2. Strong, James. *Strong's Exhaustive Concordance of the Bible*. Abingdon Press, 1890. https://biblehub.com/greek/4043.htm

Chapter 2:
Live Under His Blessing!

(7 Devotional Readings)

Rain or Shine

We held an outdoor worship service on a mid-September evening at Living Hope Church. We planned out the service in advance: Dave would lead worship, I would host, James would preach the sermon, and Pastor Mark would pray for James and his message.

As I look back on that evening, I think of other outdoor events that I have been a part of in the past. Sometimes, there would be complications with inclement weather and a storm would hinder the event and even cancel it.

Thankfully, the weather on the evening of our outdoor worship service was picturesque: perfect temperature, beautiful scenery, and the right amount of sunlight poking through the treetops before dusk. One of the funniest things about last night was that I was so at peace about the event that I never even checked the weather forecast in the days leading up to the event. Part of that might have to do with the "rain or shine" attitude that I was brought up with. My family of origin and I used to go to a Christian camp called *Camp Lebanon* in central Minnesota, and the camp director (Bill) would make sure that all of the events were lots of fun, even when they had to be modified or moved indoors. He even had a mantra: "weather is an attitude."

I have memories of walking into the outdoor amphitheater on rainy mornings and Bill would give a warm welcome. He would tell people if the Minnesota Twins baseball team won or lost, and then we would raise the American flag up the flagpole. He would then give a few reminders about the group activities that would be taking place that day. Bill made sure to mention what the plan would be for outdoor options and indoor activities. He wasn't going to let a little rain stop him (or the camp attendees) from having fun. *And he instilled that mindset in the people that were there.* Obviously, his method worked because the lesson stuck with me. Bill taught me to not let inclement weather stop me from having a great day. During every Family Camp I went to, Bill always made sure that quality family time was going to take place **rain or shine**. After all, <u>weather is an attitude</u>.

There is a powerful verse in the psalms that speaks to the concept of approaching every day with gladness because it is a day that has been graciously given by God. The verse is Psalm 118:24.

This is the day the Lord has made; let us rejoice and be glad in it.[1]

Notice that the verse says "this is the day." It doesn't say tomorrow or yesterday. The Lord wants us to take joy in the fact that He has given us **today**. Don't gloss over that last sentence. The God of the universe wants us to take joy in the fact that He made another day on this planet for us to enjoy His blessings.

I've met a lot of people who spend a lot of time planning the fun they are going to have in the future. Don't get me wrong, I think it's great to plan and it's great to look forward to coming attractions. But sometimes I wonder if so much time is being spent on planning something coming up next month that we forget to enjoy the next minutes and hours. The healthiest people I've met (and the strongest Christians I've met) are able to take joy in **today**. They are not worried about the future and they are not spending too much time dwelling on the past.

It makes sense that God would instruct us to focus on today and rejoice in it because the past is over and tomorrow hasn't happened yet. Therefore, today is all we really have. All in all, the best advice we can glean from our theme verse is that we should rejoice in today and be glad in it because it has been lovingly made by our awesome God.

Here are some basic (yet profound) principles that are good take-home thoughts for this verse.

1. This is the day - There is a connection between this Psalm and the Hebrew Passover. During Old Testament times, they were singing about God's deliverance from the bondage of Egyptians, but now we sing about Christ delivering us from the bondage of sin.

2. the Lord has made - God made everything in our world. Genesis 1:1 says, "In the beginning God created the heavens and the earth." He sustains the universe by His power and He has placed us on this earth to love Him and glorify Him.

3. let us rejoice and be glad in it. - You can enjoy all the little things in your day to the glory of God. Enjoy the sunshine and the flowers. Enjoy trees and the grass. You should definitely enjoy your family and people in your community. And this reminds us that we should _thank God for another day_ on this earth and _be glad and express joy_ as we go about our day.

---

1. *The Holy Bible: New International Version*. Colorado Springs: International Bible Society, 1984. Print.

Connect through Conversation

Our society is so distracted nowadays due to the many devices that we have. With all the screens that entertain us and take up our time, we may find that we are neglecting to have meaningful conversations with the people we care about.

My goal today is to help us step away from the screen and *take time to chat with family and friends.* You may say, "Is chit-chat with friends and family really all that important?" And my reply would be that it is *absolutely vital.*

When you chat with a friend you may just be talking about little things from the highways and byways of life, but what you are really doing is ***connecting through conversation.***

As we drive down to the road of life with our loved ones, we need to connect with them on a regular basis. Share your thoughts and feelings with them. Talk about fun memories, and dream about fun activities (or vacations) that you could do together in the future.

The simple task of planning an upcoming trip to the park (or outing at the pool) can be a fun conversation. You may talk with your children about the details of their "school life" and anticipate the upcoming school year with them.

These are all meaningful conversations, so be diligent to declutter distractions and make space for these connections.

As you buckle up and go down the road of conversation with your friends and families, take note of these *3 posted road signs* that will help you on your journey. They are all from the Book of Proverbs.

Use... **gracious words.**

"Gracious words are a honeycomb, sweet to the soul and healing to the bones." (16:24)

Use... **gentle words.**

"A gentle answer turns away wrath, but a harsh word stirs up anger." (15:1)

Use... **good timing.**

"A person finds joy in giving an apt reply—and how good is a timely word!" (15:23)

What a joy it is to connect in conversation! This is especially true in regards to connecting with our family members and close friends. There is no replacement for it!

And although talking in person is the best way to connect, don't hesitate to utilize technology. I've noticed that short conversations on the phone *can go a long way*. I know that my mom and dad love to hear from me even if it's a conversation that only lasts a few minutes.

"Quick check-in calls" allow the person who received the call to get back to what they were doing prior to taking the call. The *quick call* also allows you to "quit while you're ahead" because once you've connected for a few minutes, sometimes the appropriate thing to do is to bid them farewell. And you can certainly check in with them again in the coming days and weeks.

So, no matter if the conversation is in person or over the phone, make sure that you are staying connected with the people in your life. You just might be the "touch" that they need that day.

Even if people aren't showing huge signs of being weighed down with anxiety due to all the things going on in our world, they may be dealing with low-grade anxiety (below the surface). Your kind words and the care that you show by reaching out may cheer them up quite a bit. Proverbs 12:25 affirms, "Anxiety weighs down the heart, but a kind word cheers it up."

In the recent days, I have enjoyed some great conversations with my wife and children. But I'm not going to stop there! I'm going to try to make even deeper connections with them in the coming days, weeks, months, and years.

Would you join me in this emphasis? Will you make a renewed effort to connect through conversation with the people in your life?

Let's all take a drive down the road of conversation! Enjoy the ride with your family and friends today!

Strong Roots

I used to go on canoeing expeditions with my dad in the summer. One of my favorites was the *Canoe Race* on the Kickapoo River in southwestern Wisconsin. These are fond memories that I cherish. I thought it was pretty cool as an elementary school boy that I was in a canoe race. My dad and I didn't win, but we held our own.

In one particular year, the water was low and newly fallen branches were blocking the waterway. We would often be blocked by debris and have to portage our canoe on land around the blockade. It's safe to say that my dad did most of the carrying of the canoe, but we had a great time!

It was on those early canoe trips that I noticed a masterful sight that has never left my mind. I saw several large trees that were planted on the banks of the river. The root system was visible, and it was massive and intricate. I noticed that those "riverside" trees had a direct supply of water, and they looked healthy and strong. The picture of a riverside tree that stuck in my head through all these years is actually a picture used in the Bible. I found four great scriptures about strong roots, and two of them directly reference a tree on the river bank that puts its roots into the water. These trees don't have problems during a drought because they are directly plugged into a source of life. When we draw near to God through prayer and the deep water of His Word, we are able to more deeply understand God's love and trust Him more completely.

Check out these four principles and scriptures about strong roots. Being deeply rooted will help you stand against the winds of life and the dry times of difficulty.

1. Be rooted in God's law (His Word). Psalm 1:2-3 says, *"But his delight is in the law of the Lord, and on His law he meditates day and night. He is like a tree planted by streams of water, which yields its fruit in season and whose leaf does not wither. Whatever he does prospers."*[1]

2. Be rooted in trusting Him. Jeremiah 17:7-8 states, *"But blessed is the one who trusts in the LORD, whose confidence is in him. They will be like a tree planted by the water that sends out its roots by the stream. It does not fear when heat comes; its leaves are always green. It has no worries in a year of drought and never fails to bear fruit."*

3. Be rooted in God's love. Ephesians 3:17b-19 says, *"And I pray that you, being rooted and established in love, may have power, together with all the Lord's holy people, to grasp how wide and long and high and deep is the love of Christ, and to know this love that surpasses knowledge—that you may be filled to the measure of all the fullness of God."*

4. Be rooted and built up in Christ. Colossians 2:6-7 states, *"So then, just as you received Christ Jesus as Lord, continue to live your lives in him, rooted and built up in him, strengthened in the faith as you were taught, and overflowing with thankfulness."*

Wow! What powerful scriptures! And what a picture it is of what our lives should be.

My dad and I went back to southwestern Wisconsin for a canoe race when I was a college student. Thankfully, we didn't have to portage, but it was nice to be out by the trees and the water with my dad (who has become my friend).

As I think back to that day, I now think of a phrase that captures the essence of a deeply rooted tree on the river bank. **<u>When we have strong roots we will bear much fruit</u>**.

Being deeply rooted in Christ is the only way to thrive and grow as a Christian. A strong root system will help you help in many ways because you are cultivating a life connected to God.

Some folks find that when trouble comes they are struggling to survive while others are able to handle times of drought.

How about in your life? Have you experienced a drought recently? Are you drawing near to God and experiencing His life in season and out of season?

I pray that you will have strong roots and bear much fruit even during uncertain times. I encourage you to put your roots down deeper in Christ today, and go out and live "on mission" for Him. Show the world the fruit of a life that is vitally connected to our risen Lord!

———

1. *The Holy Bible: New International Version*. Colorado Springs: International Bible Society, 1984. Print.

Reach

I spoke with a man today who has a heart for reaching his city with the love of God. He is beginning to "think outside the box" about ways he can make an impact in his community. I enjoyed hearing his heart, and I am glad that he emphasized getting "outside of our comfort zone."

As I thought a little more about that providential conversation, I ended up thinking about how we need to **relate** to people and **reach** out to them. Many people are hurting and they can experience encouragement if we reach out to them with a *cheerful heart*. In the Book of Acts, there was much rejoicing and gladness because of what God was doing in the midst of the early believers. I would be willing to guess that their joy was contagious. Look at what it says in Acts 2.

"Every day they continued to meet together in the temple courts. They broke bread in their homes and ate together with glad and sincere hearts, praising God and enjoying the favor of all the people. And the Lord added to their number daily those who were being saved." (Acts 2:46-47)

These early believers were experiencing joy and fellowship in the Lord and were therefore in a good position to be used by the Lord to bring people into the family of God. May it be that we are used by the Lord in a similar way!

Perhaps you want to reach out more in your community but you don't know where to start. My advice would be to take a small step forward today (or this week). I believe that there are opportunities right in front of us and as we take small steps forward we can build confidence. As your confidence increases, you will find ways to relate to more members of your community. *A kind word or a helping hand can go a long way.* I came up with an acronym that will remind all of us to REACH out in our own communities.

Relate and

Extend an

Arm with a

Cheerful

Heart

When we relate to others and extend an arm with a cheerful heart, God will open doors for His Word to be shared. Perhaps you'll share a Bible verse or a story from your life. Other times you may invite them to worship with you at church. One of the most powerful tools in your toolbox is your personal testimony.

As you spend time talking with your new friend(s), make sure to *ask them about their story*. Ask them about their family and their line of work. Listen and follow up with additional questions and comments. <u>Wonderful connections can happen when people take time to share with each other about their lives.</u>

Allow me to share a few more "joy" verses from Acts as we close out this post. Joy was a marker of the apostles even during intense ministry...

Acts 5:41, *"The apostles left the Sanhedrin, rejoicing because they had been counted worthy of suffering disgrace for the Name."*

Acts 13:51, *"And the disciples were filled with joy and with the Holy Spirit."*

As you share the message of God's love with others, when (if) they accept the Lord as their Savior they will overflow with joy. In Acts 8 we see people respond positively to the ministry of Philip and they immediately rejoice!

Acts 8:8, *"So there was great joy in that city."*

Acts 8:39, *" When they came up out of the water, the Spirit of the Lord suddenly took Philip away, and the eunuch did not see him again, but went on his way rejoicing."*

You can be a Philip in your community! I hope that you'll be a game-changer (*a mover and a shaker*) in your city.

So, whether you are in your comfort zone or outside your comfort zone, make sure you **relate with others** and **extend an arm with a cheerful heart**. May your confidence and joy increase as reach out to people in your community!

Memorizing Scripture

The practice of memorizing Scripture is something that has bolstered Christians for centuries. There are many groups of believers who still prioritize memorizing Scripture today.

One of those groups is a children's program called Awana. I am so thankful that I got to be part of Awana when I was in elementary school. And I am thrilled that my children and their friends get to participate in Awana on Wednesday nights at a local Christian school called Lighthouse.

I find it interesting that as modern-day Christians, we seem to prioritize Scripture memorization for children but we leave it by the wayside in adulthood. I totally understand the aspect of getting Scripture into young minds...I love it, actually, but I don't think that the practice of memorizing Bible verses should stop once we enter adulthood.

Perhaps we need to refresh ourselves on all the benefits of memorizing Scripture and then that may motivate us to re-engage with this helpful exercise.

I thought of eight benefits to memorizing Bible verses and each one is backed by Scripture. I think you will be surprised at how valuable it is... the lost art of hiding God's word in our heart (See Psalm 119:11a).

Memorizing Scripture helps me...

Meditate on the Word of God. *"But his delight is in the law of the Lord, and on his law he meditates day and night."*[1] -Psalm 1:2

Encourage others with the Word of God. *"For everything that was written in the past was written to teach us, so that through the endurance taught in the Scriptures and the encouragement they provide we might have hope."* -Romans 15:4

Mature in the Word of God. *"Until we all reach unity in the faith and in the knowledge of the Son of God and become mature, attaining to the whole measure of the fullness of Christ."* -Ephesians 4:13

Obey the Word of God. *"But if anyone obeys His word, love for God is truly made complete in them."* -1 John 2:5a

Respect the Word of God. *"And the words of the Lord are flawless, like silver purified in a crucible, like gold refined seven times."* -Psalm 12:6

Increase in the Word of God. *"But grow in the grace and knowledge of our Lord and Savior Jesus Christ."* -2 Peter 3:18a

Be zealous for the Word of God. *"Never be lacking in zeal, but keep your spiritual fervor, serving the Lord."* -Romans 12:11

Enjoy the Word of God. *"The precepts of the Lord are right, giving joy to the heart. The commands of the Lord are radiant, giving light to the eyes."* -Psalm 19:8

What great reasons to memorize various verses of the Bible! When we are built up in Scripture, we are in a better position to be used by God.

You may not have noticed yet, but the eight reasons to memorize Scripture form a helpful acrostic: M.E.M.O.R.I.Z.E.

When we hide God's Word in our heart, we can more easily **meditate** on His Word and **encourage** others with His Word. As we **mature** and **obey** in His Word, we grow to **respect** and **increase** in His Word with **zeal** and **enjoyment**.

Let's all be people that M.E.M.O.R.I.Z.E. God's Word! It doesn't have to be complicated. Start with one verse today!

Perhaps you'll review verses you had committed to memory when you were younger. As you brush up on the passages that you had previously memorized, a lot of it will come back to your mind. God's Word is powerful and sharper than any two-edged sword! (See Heb. 4:12)

It's no wonder the psalmist writes, "I have hidden your word in my heart that I might not sin against you." (Ps. 119:11)

May you be built up as you commit various verses to memory! And may you encourage others with the Scripture that has been stored up in your heart!

---

1. *The Holy Bible: New International Version*. Colorado Springs: International Bible Society, 1984. Print.

Blue Zip Up

When I was in elementary school, I used to go for walks with my grandpa around the park near his house. My grandpa's name was Lyle and walking around the park (which was a one-mile loop) was part of his daily regimen. We both enjoyed our special times together.

There were many sights and sounds on the trail at this beautiful park in Roseville, Minnesota. There were many other trail walkers that we would see while walking around Lake Bennett which is situated in the heart of the park. We would look out at the ducks that were swimming out on the lake.

There were beautiful leaves in the fall and we would trounce over those wet leaves on a soggy October day. There were brisk spring days that were much appreciated after a long cold winter. We would get out on the paved trail and enjoy the warmer spring air as we embarked on an invigorating hike.

The summer hikes were probably the best and we would see the sun glistening off the lake.

My grandpa was a man of outstanding character and he loved his family very much. He grew in his walk with the Lord throughout his life. There is a verse in Scripture that I read this morning that reminded me of my grandpa.

The verse is 2 Thessalonians 1:3. Let's read it together.

We ought always to thank God for you, brothers and sisters, and rightly so, because your faith is growing more and more, and the love all of you have for one another is increasing.

This verse shows us three **biblical attributes** that we should practice in our life. If we practice these things in our lives, we will experience the blessing of God.

1. Thankfulness *We ought always to thank God for you, brothers and sisters,...* (v. 3a)

Cultivating a thankful heart will do wonders for your walk with God. Thank Him for what He's done for you in Christ and thank Him for all He has given you.

2. Faith *...and rightly so, because your faith is growing more and more,...* (v. 3b)

This verse talks about a growing faith, so make sure that you lean into the Lord on a daily basis. He will help you grow. He helps us in all things, and He wants all of us to grow into fully mature believers.

3. Love *...and the love all of you have for one another is increasing.* (v. 3c)

Increasing in love for our brothers and sisters in the faith is shown through acts of kindness. We love others because we are loved so deeply by God. As you go forward, ask God to increase your love for others and then show people your love through your actions.

My grandpa grew in all of these things and you can too. Grandpa Lyle always wore a smile on his face and he always wore a blue zip up jacket on a spring or fall day on his daily walk. He liked wearing his blue zip up so much that he had to purchase more than one. He had several of them hanging in his closet near the front door of his house.

We would lace up the shoes, zip up the jacket, and head out for a hike that was filled with joy and peace. Lyle would spread his joy by saying "hello" to other people on the trail but we had a lot of joy by just being together in God's creation as grandfather and grandson.

Perhaps you'll take a nature hike today and enjoy a trail near your house. Don't forget to dress for the weather. But, most importantly, remember to put on **thankfulness, faith, and love**.

These are the attributes that God wants us to increase in. Jesus modeled all three of these traits for us, and His sacrificial death on the cross is the only reason that we can partake in all three.

May you grow in all of these biblical attributes! ....increasing in thankfulness, growing in faith, and showing love to others.

The Power of Forgiveness

Some people are quick to forgive, others hold on to grudges. I have observed many people through the years who fall into both of these categories. And before we get into the spiritual aspect of forgiveness, I want to take a moment to point out my personal observations of people who forgive and people who don't forgive.

People who forgive walk a little lighter.

People who don't forgive carry extra weight on their shoulders.

People who forgive smile more easily.

People who don't forgive develop frown lines more quickly.

People who forgive laugh often.

People who don't forgive complain often.

People who forgive feel free to dance.

People who don't forgive are a little more stiff.

These are simply my observations (and generalizations), but don't miss the key point: **forgiveness is freeing.** But why is it so hard for people to do? I think it's because we don't fully understand what forgiveness is.

Perhaps someone has wronged you and you think that if you forgive them, you are letting them off the hook. However, the opposite is true. You want to keep that person on the hook (and not forgive them), but the person who's actually hooked is you. The unforgiveness that you have chosen as your mode of operation has actually latched its hooks into you. And now you are trapped in a box of resentment, bondage, and unforgiveness.

I only say this to help everyone who is reading this to choose forgiveness instead of unforgiveness. Withholding forgiveness will eat at you. It will rob you.

But the good news is... when we forgive, relationships are restored! It's awesome! *Two friends being fully reconciled. A husband and wife being back on good terms and back in each other's arms.* What a vital thing forgiveness is!

God forgave us. Amen! That's why we forgive. He gave His Son on the cross for our sins. And now we extend forgiveness to others because we've been forgiven.

I was in the sanctuary of my church yesterday as I began to think about forgiveness, and I eventually thought of the concept of the **ABC's of Forgiveness**. There are *three movements* that you need to take if you need to apologize to someone.

A – Approach the person you wronged (gently).

B – Be clear in admitting where you were wrong.

C – Communicate that you are sorry and ask for their forgiveness.

If you simply will follow these basic steps, I trust that you will keep solid (reconciled) relationships in your life. Paul writes in Ephesians 4:32, "Be kind and compassionate to one another, forgiving each other, just as in Christ God forgave you."

Forgiveness is not optional. God is very clear with us that we need to be *forgiving people*. Matthew 6:12 says (Jesus speaking), "And forgive us our debts, as we also have forgiven our debtors." Being someone who forgives is a mark of a Christian.

We can admit when we're wrong and we can graciously offer forgiveness to others because we have been forgiven so profoundly (and completely) in Christ.

You will probably need to make the first move. *Move toward* your friend. *Move toward* your co-worker or family member. *Move toward* your spouse (if you are married).

So, how can you put into practice what we learned today?

Don't hold a grudge. May we all be quick to forgive and quick to say "I'm sorry."

You'll be glad you did. And your relationships will be better for it.

Chapter 3:
<u>Lighten your Load!</u>

(7 Devotional Readings)

Cast your Cares

I've been able to connect with a lot of people in central Missouri, and I've noticed that there is a regular theme in the conversation. People are worried. Don't get me wrong; they are happy about the positive things that are going on in their life, but with all the events going in the world they have fears bubbling up from below the surface.

There have been wildfires on the west coast that have been devasting to many areas. A lady from my church that I spoke with recently was very unsettled about the wildfires. She was concerned about all of the fallout because the disastrous fires are taking people's homes and causing mass evacuation.

I noticed that she had implemented a very important Biblical tactic to calm her concerns. She did something positive with her angst. **She prayed.** Actually, she shared with me that she has a _dedicated prayer time_ every morning to lift her requests before the Lord. Her emphasis on regular prayer is a phenomenal example of casting one's cares on God.

The verse that is on my mind today is 1 Peter 5:7. This short power-packed verse of Scripture is a theme verse for me this week and I feel privileged to share it with you. Even if you've heard this passage before, I encourage you to experience it today with an open mind and a willingness to hear from God in a fresh way.

Cast all your anxiety on Him because He cares for you. (1 Peter 5:7)

As I pondered the implications of this verse, it got me thinking that we have a **responsibility** to cast our cares on Him. We can't rely on someone else to do it for us. Yes, we can receive wise counsel from a helpful friend (I highly recommend it), but then we need to do what God is calling us to do... cast our cares on Him.

Casting our cares literally means that we need to *throw* our concerns and worries off of us and onto God. He can handle it. He can take them! Nothing is too hard for God!

As you throw your cares onto God it will probably feel like a burden is being lifted from your shoulders... well... because a burden is being lifted from your shoulders. Don't let worries weigh you down and cause you to have a heavy heart. Lighten your load!

The primary way that we cast our cares on God is **prayer**.

Philippians 4:6-7 makes it clear that we should pray instead of going down the road of worry.

Do not be anxious about anything, but in every situation, by prayer and petition, with thanksgiving, present your requests to God. And the peace of God, which transcends all understanding, will guard your hearts and your minds in Christ Jesus.

Some people have made it their habit to worry about everything in life and they feel it's their responsibility to take on other people's worries, too. On the flip side, other people have made it their habit to pray about the things that they're concerned about and they are free to pray about the difficulties that other people are facing, too. See the difference? When we acknowledge that God cares for us and that He carefully watches over us, it makes it easier to throw our worries upon Him. When we are leaning into a close relationship with Him, it is the logical step that we would cast our cares upon our loving Father.

Since my goal was that we would have a fresh encounter with our theme verse today, I am going to let the verse be our main takeaway points. I trust that it will encourage you to lighten your load and rest in His love.

1. Cast all your anxiety on Him

(Cast all your anxieties, worries, and concerns)[1]

2. because He cares for you.

(He cares with deepest affection. He watches over you very carefully.)[2]

Throw your cares and worries onto the Lord. This will enable you to walk forward with a lighter load and more joy in your heart.

---

1. *The Amplified Bible: Containing the Amplified Old Testament and the Amplified New Testament.* Grand Rapids: Zondervan, 1965. Print.

2. Ibid.

Trail Mix

I have always enjoyed hiking during the summer months. I've gone on
treks in other months of the year too, but there is something special
about doing it in the summer. The days are longer and the sun shines
brighter. You feel the warmth in the air, and if you're walking around a
lake you can look out at the water's surface and see it glistening.

If you're only going on a short hike you probably just need a hat and
some good walking shoes. However, if you're going on a longer journey
I have found that taking **water** is absolutely essential to beat the heat
and taking **trail mix** isn't a bad idea either.

It is fun to be able to stop at a midpoint on the trail and open up a bag
of gorp (fancy word for trail mix). You reach your hand into the bag and
grin as you prepare for your tasty "energy snack." You know that the
mix of raisins, peanuts, M&Ms, almonds and cashews will provide you
with a boost. And it is just altogether fun to eat trail mix while you're
out enjoying a hike. You may even find a well-placed bench on the trail
as a perfect haven to enjoy your power-packed snack.

Something as simple as *trail mix* got me thinking about what things we
need to take with us on the path of life and what things we need to leave
by the wayside.

I was reading segments of the longest psalm today (Psalm 119), and I
walked right into two things that are essential for the journey. I also
noticed two treacherous pathways that need to be avoided.

Take along... His commands.

"Direct me in the path of your commands, for there I find delight."
(v. 35)

Don't take... the corrupt pathway.

*"I have kept my feet from every evil path so that I might obey your
word."* (v. 101)

Take along... illumination devices. (His Word!)

"Your word is a lamp for my feet, a light on my path." (v. 105)

Don't take... the incorrect pathway.

"Because I love your commands more than gold, more than pure gold, and because I consider all your precepts right, I hate every wrong path." (v. 127-128)

Why is it that so many people find themselves on a pathway that is harmful for their life? Why is it that so many people don't take along the right things for the journey? We need God's Word! We need His commands! He wants us to have a successful journey on the path of life, so He counsels us on which way to go and He keeps His loving eye on us. Psalm 32:8 says, "I will instruct you and teach you in the way you should go; I will counsel you with my loving eye on you."

You don't need to be weighed down with anxiety as you journey through life. God will help you feel lighter and He'll even put a spring in your step if you'll just give your burdens to Him.

I've gone on long hikes up 14,000 ft. mountains... sometimes I carried a backpack and other times I didn't have a backpack. I can attest that the hike is easier and the difficult steps are more navigable when I don't have a backpack weighing me down.

You may need to lighten your load in life. If you're carrying burdens and worries, consider jettisoning them on the side of the path. Just bring the essentials: 1) the loving commands of God, 2) the flashlight of His Word, and I would add number 3) a friend for the journey.

That friend may even be willing to carry part of your load when you can't carry it anymore.

As we wrap up, allow me to encourage you to dig deep into God's Word in the coming weeks. Maybe you'll spend some time in the Psalms. And as you spend time in the Bible, make sure you do your best to apply God's truth to your life. We stay on His pathway "by living according to [His] Word." (See Psalm 119:9)

You'll be thankful that you took the right things on your journey and stayed on the correct pathway in the *walk of life.*

Streams in the Desert

Life can be pretty tiring sometimes. During difficult times, you may feel worse than tired because you feel disappointed or disoriented. One person I spoke with expressed that moving from one part of the country to another can be very disorienting. He moved from Wisconsin to Missouri and regularly used the word *disorienting* to describe his experience. Even when God seems to have blessed a situation (of transition or moving) you may still find yourself feeling disappointed or disoriented at times.

I spoke with an 18 year-old at our youth gathering last night, and she shared about how she is getting ready for college after graduating from high school. She showed some real wisdom by expressing how she is going into college with strong friendships and good family relationships (and she even found a church in her college town). She indicated that this will help her feel less disoriented and alone. BINGO!

In the Book of Isaiah, Isaiah is writing to the Israelites in anticipation of their exile to Babylon and then pointing to how they will leave Babylon and come back to Judah. He uses imagery from the *exodus from Egypt* to show how the Israelites were literally going to experience a "second exodus" as they leave Babylon and go back to Judah. Isaiah knew that as the people left Babylon and went back to the Promised Land, they would need a vision to see past the desolate wasteland that it had become. He knew that some of the Israelites would feel disappointed and disoriented as they came back to a place that had been reduced to rubble (the temple was destroyed).

But God says...

See, I am doing a new thing!
  Now it springs up; do you not perceive it?
I am making a way in the wilderness
  and streams in the wasteland. (Isaiah 43:19)

As God's people, we need to have a vision for the restoration that God wants to bring in any particular situation. As the Israelites obeyed God, they were able to see that He was indeed doing a new thing. God was bringing life to a lifeless situation. He was bringing a time of renewal to His people in the land He had promised.

What about in your life? What vision has God put in your heart to bring restoration to a particular situation? Maybe He has put multiple things on your heart and mind. Perhaps you want to have a purposeful next twelve months as you make healthy choices and build solid relationships. You may have a vision to bring people together in a small group or support group so that you can all grow together. Perhaps God is guiding you to reach out to folks who are hurting. Maybe you want to start a new initiative or a new organization.

I don't know what your situation is, but I know that you should not shrivel up and back down in fear. Notice what God says in our theme verse: "Behold, I am doing a new thing."

We all have to be prepared for new things, because **change** is something that is happening constantly around us. It is a part of life.

And folks, we need to move on from the things of the past. Look at the verse prior to our theme verse. Verse 18 says, "Forget the former things; do not dwell on the past." Don't let things in the rear-view mirror distract you from driving ahead in life.

Isaiah 43:18-19 applies to us as New Testament believers as well, because we are looking forward to a New Jerusalem as we await our eternal home with the Lord. "I am doing a new thing" from Isaiah 43 sounds quite similar to what Jesus says in Revelation 21:5... "I am making everything new!"

You can pursue your dreams and your goals (or whatever God is calling you to do) because you have a solid foundation in Christ. He is our Cornerstone. Ephesians 2:20b says, "Christ Jesus himself as the chief cornerstone."

You don't have to worry about all the little fears of life. Shake those off! You are secure in Him, and you should press forward in your pursuit of the goals that have been laid on your heart. Maybe you need to increase your vision and seek to broaden your influence. God will help you see that streams can begin to flow even in an area of your life that looks like a desert.

So as we wrap up, let me give you a few do's and don'ts and an admonition to move ahead.

1. DON'T look back. (v. 18)

2. DO look up. (v. 19a)

3. DO look forward with fresh vision. (v. 19)

4. Move forward, relying on God. (v. 19b)

Let It Go!

18

As you read the title of this post, you may think that I'm trying to do my best impression of Elsa from a popular cold-weather movie. Sorry to disappoint you, but that is not the case. Although I do like belting out the chorus of the *Frozen* theme-song, this post is about the all-important exchange of forgiveness.

When you forgive someone, you are essentially ***letting it go***. You are making a decision and an affirmation that you are not going to hold onto that offense any longer.

Forgiveness is such an important topic that I feel like it should be talked about on a regular basis. I can't think of a concept as important as forgiveness as it pertains to preserving the health of a marriage or a friendship.

Let's face the facts, people get offended. When the offended party is disgruntled (*or just plain gruntled*) after the offense takes place, how do we navigate that impasse? How do we mend that broken bridge?

The answer is simple. **Forgiveness.**

An exchange like this needs to take place...

Person A: "I'm sorry. What I did was wrong. Please forgive me."

Person B: "I forgive you."

Notice how person B says "I forgive you." That is important. Don't miss that! She doesn't simply say, "Ah shucks, it's okay" because it wasn't okay that person A did something sinful to person B. It's vital that the person says, "I forgive you" because that is the act of releasing the person and letting it go. You are not holding onto the offense any longer and you are officially letting them off the hook. **Forgiveness has been granted and you are on good terms again.**

Forgiveness will do wonders for your heart (spiritually). People care a lot about physical heart health, but we also need to pay attention to spiritual heart health.

Forgiveness is one of the first prescriptions that a pastor should give you for your spiritual health.

Being a person who forgives is so healthy for your heart that I made a list of 7 things that forgiveness does for you. So, here is the list...

If you F.O.R.G.I.V.E. people consistently, it will help you keep a...

Free heart (Matt. 6:14)

Obedient heart (Col. 3:13)

Respectful heart (Matt. 6:12)

Gentle heart (Eph. 4:32)

Inclusive heart (Luke 6:37)

Vibrant heart (Prov. 10:12)

Eager heart (Mark 11:25)

I only put the verse references in there so that you have the opportunity to open up your Bible and look at these verses about forgiveness. However, allow me to share three of the verses with you right now.

Matthew 6:14 (Jesus speaking), *"For if you forgive other people when they sin against you, your heavenly Father will also forgive you."*

Colossians 3:13, *"Bear with each other and forgive one another if any of you has a grievance against someone. Forgive as the Lord forgave you."*

Ephesians 4:32, *"Be kind and compassionate to one another, forgiving each other, just as in Christ God forgave you."*

These are powerful Scriptures that show the high importance of forgiveness. Since we have been forgiven by God in Christ by what He did for us on the cross, how can we not offer forgiveness to one another?

Fish Out of Water

19

In 2015 when I was living in Wisconsin, I remember officiating a youth soccer game during the fall season. My father-in-law (Larry) lived near the soccer complex and while the game was going on I saw him walking on the paved pathway near the soccer field and he waved to me. The reason that this stood out to me so much was that he was bundled up in a winter coat on a moderate fall day in central Wisconsin.

Larry looked like a *fish out of water* with his extreme wardrobe choice. He grew up in the country of Panama and he appreciates warm weather and despises cold weather. When he was 39, God called him and his family to move from Texas to Wisconsin to plant a church. Once Larry hit the age of 52, I began to notice that he was out of his element in regards to the cold weather in Wisconsin. I knew that it was only a matter of time until he and his wife started looking for a place to live that was south of the "Badger State."

Sure enough, Larry and his wife moved down to Missouri in 2016 to lead a church in Hermann, MO. My family and I followed suit in 2017 as I took a job as a *Director of Family Ministries* in Jefferson City, MO. Thankfully, Larry doesn't look like a fish out of water anymore, and we are all enjoying life in Missouri. Both of our families know that we are at the church that God has called us to be.

The concept of someone feeling like a **fish out of water** got me thinking… There are many people that I have met who seem to feel like they will be a fish out of water if they do projects with other churches who are somewhat different than theirs. I think some of this is simply the human bent toward familiarity. However, the other aspect is that many believers *sadly* choose not to pursue unity in regards to co-laboring with other denominations in ministry work and service projects. Why do many believers make this negative decision? I think one of the reasons is that they think that they will be *compromising* if they pursue a unifying endeavor with a group that has "debatable" doctrine. But here is the truth that can dispel that myth: we can have **unity without compromise.** Psalm 133:1 says, "How good and pleasant it is when God's people live together in unity!"

We need to look for ways to be unified, not dis-unified. You can have unity without compromise. Psalm 133 says that it is **good** and **pleasant** to cultivate unity! We should not gloss over those words. We could conversely say that it is **not good** and **not pleasant** when brothers make a deliberate choice not to be unified. We can have *real* unity because of what Jesus did on the cross for us. He broke down the dividing wall between Jew and Gentile through His blood being shed for us. (See Ephesians 2:13) **All of us stand on level ground at the foot of the cross**; forgiven and free. We have been saved by grace through faith! (See Ephesians 2:8) We are free to serve with our fellow Christian brothers and sisters because we are one in Christ, and we should make every effort to remove barriers between our different groups. As we remove barriers, more partnerships between different denominations for gospel ministry and service work will take place. I believe that these partnerships to serve the Lord together truly do bring glory to God.

It's okay that we don't believe the same exact thing on non-essential doctrines. Don't get hung up on those differences! Acknowledge that we're all one in Christ. This brings much joy to the heart when you're with believers who are different than you. What you end up realizing is that you have *a lot in common*. And the most important connection we all have with everyone else in the Body of Christ is our **common faith**. As long as another group preaches salvation through faith in Christ, you should not have qualms about serving with that group. Yes, I'm sure there are situations that could exist in which separating is necessary, but those are the exception, not the rule. We definitely should use wisdom, but above all we need to walk in charity, respect, and cooperation. Let's do this!

As we wrap up, I also want us to look at verse 3 of this psalm. Psalm 133:3 says, "It is as if the dew of Hermon were falling on Mount Zion. For there the Lord bestows His blessing, even life forevermore." My Study Bible says, "The dew [of Hermon] is crucial for the vegetation during the dry season, and the image conveys the thought of a fruitful land."[1] This verse clearly shows us that unity can be very fruitful. I love that image! I hope that we all pursue unity with a gracious heart and that we all experience the fruitfulness in ministry that God provides when unity is cultivated.

You don't have to feel like a fish out of water anymore; get out and serve with other believers in your community! Here are two take-aways as you go!

1. Christian unity is *good and pleasant*. (v. 1)

2. Christian unity is *fruitful*. (v. 3)

———

1. *ESV: Study Bible. English Standard Version.* Wheaton, Ill: Crossway Bibles, 2007. Print.

Worrying Doesn't Work

20

Jesus said, "Who of you by worrying can add a single hour to your life?" (Matthew 6:27)

This verse articulates a basic truth... ***worrying doesn't work.***

I was reading in Matthew chapter 6 today, and I stumbled across some principles and tactics to help us in the battle against worry.

I call it *the list of things to do instead of worrying*. It's safe to say that it's not a catchy title, but it's a "working title" and it's all I have right now. Work with me people!!

So let's get down to the *List*! All of the points on the list come from Matthew 6 and Philippians 4.

1. Instead of worrying... *trust in God's provision.*

"Therefore I tell you, do not worry about your life, what you will eat or drink; or about your body, what you will wear. Is not life more than food, and the body more than clothes? Look at the birds of the air; they do not sow or reap or store away in barns, and yet your heavenly Father feeds them." (Matthew 6:25-26)

2. Instead of worrying... *acknowledge that God knows your situation.*

"Who of you by worrying can add a single hour to your life? And why do you worry about clothes? See how the flowers of the field grow. They do not labor or spin. Yet I tell you that not even Solomon in all his splendor was dressed like one of these. If that is how God clothes the grass of the field, which is here today and tomorrow is thrown into the fire, will he not much more clothe you—you of little faith? "So do not worry saying 'What shall we eat?' or 'What shall we drink?' or 'What shall we wear?' For the pagans run after these things, and your heavenly Father knows that you need them." (Matthew 6:27-32)

3. Instead of worrying... *seek His kingdom and His righteousness.*

"But seek first his kingdom and his righteousness, and all these things will be given to you as well." (Matthew 6:33)

4. Instead of worrying... *attack the day!* (and face tomorrow as it comes.)

"Therefore do not worry about tomorrow, for tomorrow will worry about itself. Each day has enough trouble of its own." (Matthew 6:34)

5. Instead of worrying... *pray.*

"Do not be anxious about anything, but in every situation, by prayer and petition, with thanksgiving, present your requests to God. And the peace of God, which transcends all understanding, will guard your hearts and your minds in Christ Jesus." (Philippians 4:6-7)

6. Instead of worrying... *think about something else.*

"Finally, brothers, whatever is true, whatever is noble, whatever is right, whatever is pure, whatever is lovely, whatever is admirable – if anything is excellent or praiseworthy – think about such things." (Philippians 4:8)

We could sum it up by saying this: Trust the Lord and release your worries! Pray to God about your concerns and think about godly things.

Now, go out and enjoy some fresh air in your yard today! Life is too short to stay inside all day worrying.

Son of Encouragement

21

As we go through life, whether we're going through a hard year or a good year, we all need encouragement. Storms come into our life and the wind blows us around, and it's often an encouraging friend who stays by our side and keeps our head above water.

We ought to thank those "encouragers" in our lives. The act of coming alongside somebody and keeping them strong is a wonderful thing and it is not to be overlooked. When I was running a half-marathon during college there was a man I met on the course during the second half of the race who stayed by my side and encouraged me. Just his presence at my side helped me run faster. That's the picture of an encourager.

There was a man in the New Testament who was such an encourager that they gave him a name that meant Son of Encouragement.

Look at Acts 4:36-37.

"Joseph, a Levite from Cyprus, whom the apostles called Barnabas (which means son of encouragement), sold a field he owned and brought the money and put it at the apostles' feet."

This guy not only talked the talk, he walked the walk. And it gets even better. He continued to build people up as the church began to grow in different cities around the ancient world.

In Acts 9 we see him bridging the gap between Saul (later called Paul) and the apostles. Verse 26-28 describes the beautiful encouragement that Barnabas was able to provide. Let's read it together.

"When [Saul] came to Jerusalem, he tried to join the disciples, but they were all afraid of him, not believing that he really was a disciple. But Barnabas took him and brought him to the apostles. He told them how Saul on his journey had seen the Lord and that the Lord had spoken to him, and how in Damascus he had preached fearlessly in the name of Jesus. So Saul stayed with them and moved about freely in Jerusalem, speaking boldly in the name of the Lord."

It doesn't stop there. Barnabas just keeps on encouraging.

Acts 11:22b-23 says, *"They sent Barnabas to Antioch. When he arrived and saw what the grace of God had done, he was glad and encouraged them all to remain true to the Lord with all their hearts."*

Here was a guy who knew what his gift was and he was using it in full force. When he arrived on the scene in Antioch, he was able to step in there and play his God-given role. His gift of exhortation was not wasted and the words that he spoke had power because He consistently walked with the Lord. He was a man of character.

Look at how Acts 11:24a describes Barnabas.

"He was a good man, full of the Holy Spirit and faith."

So, as we look at how Barnabas conducted himself, let's now shift to present-day and apply it to our lives.

Are you regularly looking for ways to encourage people?

Are you growing spiritually and following God's Spirit in your daily life?

What are some ways you can build people up this week whether it's with words or a thoughtful gift?

Who do you need to call today? Who do you need to send a *note of encouragement* to today?

There is a three-pronged method that I see Barnabas doing throughout the Book of Acts that I want to do in my life. I want to follow his example and in some small way be a modern-day *Son of Encouragement* and I hope that you will find many ways to encourage people in your life, too.

The Barnabas Method...

See the Need ——> Meet the Need ——> Speak God's Peace

Chapter 4:
<u>Bask in God's Grace!</u>

(7 Devotional Readings)

Shepherd's Pie

22

It was a nice evening on the very last day of August and my wife and I were about to start getting the kids ready for bed. The doorbell rang and it was one of my neighbors at the door. It was a man named Gordie who lives a few houses down the street from me.

He came to show me a wood carving he had done. It was top-quality craftsmanship, but the cool thing about it was that the whole 23rd Psalm was written on it. He even made some small carving marks on the top and bottom to make it look like a scroll. Very cool!

After seeing that great plaque by Gordie, I knew I had to read Psalm 23 and I was compelled to write about it. While reading the psalm, I was struck by how the psalm opened with the word LORD and ended with the word LORD. It was as if David (the author) was trying to highlight how the Lord is preeminent and that He truly is a sovereign shepherd.

Do you need a sovereign shepherd in your life? We all do! And David makes it incredibly clear with his masterful imagery when he says, "The Lord is my shepherd." David was a shepherd for many years, so this was a description that he knew very well and he also knew that the people of the day would understand exactly what he meant when he referenced God as his shepherd.

In an agrarian society, shepherding was a common profession that required day-and-night hours. Therefore, the reader would know that God (as a shepherd) would look out for all the needs of His people through the entire day and all hours of the night.

As I thought about this psalm and how we can understand it in 2021 and in our present-day culture, I concluded that we need to think like sheep. As we think like simple, helpless sheep we will see that we do indeed need to rely on God for all of our needs. We do not have it all figured out! And we can't do it all by ourselves!

Sheep seem to understand that they need a shepherd, but we (stubborn humans) think that we can do it without a shepherd. "No thanks, God. I've got this one by myself."

As I read through this psalm, I was able to dig out some key principles that apply to our daily lives. People love to quote parts of this psalm... but *what is it saying to us* today?

Here are the three things I discovered.

1. Our Shepherd God gives us His provision.

Ps. 23:1 – *"The Lord is my shepherd, I lack nothing."*

2. Our Shepherd God gives us His peace.

Ps. 23:2 – *"He makes me lie down in green pastures, He leads me beside quiet waters."*

3. Our Shepherd God gives us His protection.

Ps. 23:4 – *"Even though I walk through the darkest valley, I will fear no evil, for you are with me; your rod and your staff, they comfort me."*

As we go through the trials of life, sometimes we focus on only one aspect of God's attributes. However, in this psalm I believe that we are shown that we can rely on His provision, His peace, and His protection all at the same time.

In other words, you don't just focus on one piece of the pie. You get the whole pie because God is with us at all times with all of His glorious attributes. I guess you could call it a shepherd's pie!

It is a mighty blessing that we have the Lord Jesus to guide us. He is the Good Shepherd (John 10:11). I encourage you to lean into His love and guidance today.

May we all experience His shepherding touch, and may we encourage one another as we walk together as the sheep of His pasture. He will **provide**, He will give **peace**, and He will **protect**.

Journey up the Mountain

23

When I was a preteen I had the privilege of hiking up the tallest
mountain in South Dakota. The mountain was called Harney Peak, and
it was a memorable hike. My dad and I enjoyed the hike together, and
in a serendipitous turn of events we ran into another father-son duo on
the trail that was from our hometown of Marshfield, WI. I guess they
had the same idea we did; enjoy some male-bonding while hiking up a
beautiful trail with spectacular views. Good times!

Several years later, our entire extended family made the trip out to
South Dakota and we made our way up Harney Peak (which was now
called Black Elk Peak). The hike didn't seem as difficult now that I was
an adult, but it was fun to share that memory with my relatives.

I remember having an encouraging conversation with my uncle Steve
on the trail that day. He provided an uplifting attitude and as I look
back on that day his positive mindset stands out.

Uncle Steve encourages our family with some thoughtful words from
the Bible every year before we partake of Thanksgiving Dinner at his
home. Psalm 24 is a scripture that comes to mind when I think about
the memorable holiday celebrations in his home and the unforgettable
hikes we've shared together in South Dakota and Colorado.

The 24th Psalm is a psalm of David and the author launches into a
"hymn of praise" and he "instructs prospective worshipers."[1] The verses
of this psalm lay out a healthy template for any believer as he or she
prepares to enter into worship. Let's look at a few of the verses.

Psalm 24:1-6 – The earth is the Lord's, and everything in it,
the world, and all who live in it;
[2] for He founded it upon the seas
and established it on the waters.
[3] Who may ascend the mountain of the Lord?
Who may stand in His holy place?
[4] The one who has clean hands and a pure heart,
who does not trust in an idol
or swear by a false god.
[5] They will receive blessing from the Lord
and vindication from God their Savior.
[6] Such is the generation of those who seek Him,
who seek Your face, God of Jacob.

Here are the key aspects that I see in this passage that instruct us in our preparation for worship.

1. Praise God for his awesome work in creation.

2. Purify your heart before God.

3. Prepare to receive the Lord's blessing through His Word.

A few years after our big family hike up Black Elk Peak, I was able to enjoy another hike with my uncle Steve. This time our hiking team consisted of a couple of my cousins, my dad, and Steve. We actually conquered three 14,000 ft. mountains on that day: 1) Mount Cameron, 2) Mount Lincoln, and 3) Mount Bross. My dad provided me with encouragement during the middle part of the hike, especially when I got a brief altitude headache at the summit of Mount Lincoln. After we topped the last of them (Mount Bross), my dad and my two cousins went ahead of me on the trail on our way down the mountain. I had the privilege of sharing the trail with good ole' uncle Steve again and we traversed the steep terrain together.

He provided encouragement, as always, and I was comforted by his patient spirit when we got to the bottom of the mountain. He was happy to have finished the hike and he gladly prepared himself to wait (for a very long time) for his wife's hiking group to come to the bottom of the mountain. He was ready to greet her when she arrived back to base-camp after a full day of hiking.

I am thankful to have such great encouragers and examples like my dad and uncle Steve in my life. The hikes are memorable, but I think the relationships that have deepened are what's most important. It is a blessing from God that we can come to worship Him with fellow believers. Many of these believers can provide encouragement to us and a positive example for us to follow.

So, here is the main idea as we wrap up today... As we prepare to worship the Lord on any occasion, it is appropriate that we do the same things that David instructed in the 24th Psalm: 1) **praise** His handiwork, 2) **purify** our hearts, and 3) **prepare** to receive His Word.

---

1. *Ryrie, Charles C. Ryrie Study Bible: New American Standard Bible, 1995 Update.* Chicago: Moody Press, 1995. Print.

Mini-Golf Madness

24

During the warmer months, one of my favorite outdoor activities is mini-golf. It provides a challenge and a friendly competitive atmosphere that I enjoy.

When my wife and I went on our honeymoon, we played mini-golf three times at a place called *Jungle Golf* in Fort Myers, Florida. They had a "discount" going on that got me excited; you only had to pay one fee and you could play as many rounds as you wanted in one day. We noticed that the course wasn't very crowded and we were able to get in three rounds on that day! What a deal!

I was enjoying my first week with my bride, and we decided that we were going to play "competitive" mini-golf; not just for fun. I thought I would be able to win since I had played a lot of mini-golf in my life, but my wife reminded me that she had played a lot too.

The results showed that Gracie and I were on an even playing field on the mini-golf course.

The three rounds went as follows: I won one round, Gracie won one round, and in another round we had the exact same score. You can't get any more even than that!

There were officially "no bragging rights" because we were locked dead even, but my wife reminded me a few times afterwards about how well she had played. She even had a hole-in-one! She knew how to focus and aim the ball properly, even when she was standing over a putt that was a far distance from the hole.

I could tell numerous stories of other mini-golf outings that I have enjoyed with my family, but one of the keys to these friendly competitions is utilizing the little scorecard that the mini-golf establishment provides. You see, sometimes people forget how many strokes they took on the last hole so this little tool helps keeps everyone on track. Usually these mistakes are accidental but sometimes it might be because they don't want to take a penalty stroke for hitting their ball in the water!

The scorecard is the official document that settles any questions or confusion about what the score is. The goal is not only to have a fun family outing but also to see who had the best day on the mini-golf course.

Mini-golf enthusiasts keep their opponents honest with the use of a scorecard, but in our spiritual life we know that we don't have to worry about God making a mistake. We have a Lord who is faithful and true! Let's look at Psalm 117. It is the shortest psalm; just two verses long!

"Praise the Lord, all nations;

Laud Him all peoples!

For His lovingkindness is great toward us,

And the truth of the Lord is everlasting.

Praise the Lord!"[1]

A New Testament verse that harmonizes well with this psalm is John 14:6a, in which Jesus says, "I am the way, the truth, and the life." Jesus is the truth and He gives us life! He is our way to the Father!

We ought to praise the Lord continually for all that He is and all that He has done. This psalm shows us some powerful things about God, and it gives us a directive.

1. God is loving and kind toward us. (This is supremely seen in what Christ did for us on the Cross.)

2. The Lord's truth is everlasting.

3. Therefore, we should praise the Lord!

The principles are basic, yet so profound! If we would reckon these "cornerstone aspects" of God on a regular basis and praise Him every day, it would honor the Lord and make a big difference in our lives. Other people would be affected too, because praising the Lord is contagious. *Passion breeds passion.*

As we wrap up today, just remember... you can have *true peace* because you know that God is loving and kind towards you. You can trust Him because His truth is everlasting. Therefore, let's praise the Lord together, not only every Sunday morning, but also as we go about our week! Amen. [So be it.]

---

1. *New American Standard Bible.* La Habra, CA: Foundation Publications, for the Lockman Foundation, 1995. Print.

Grace and Peace

25

Almost everyone I know likes receiving letters in the mail. There is something about receiving a card or a note of encouragement that can really brighten your day!

The Book of First Peter is a letter that the apostle wrote to believers about living by faith and maintaining hope, even in the midst of suffering. It is a message that all Christians need to heed.

Peter begins in verse 1 of chapter 1 by introducing himself, just as you would. He says, "[This is] *Peter, an apostle of Jesus Christ.*"

Peter goes on, "*To God's elect, exiles scattered throughout the provinces of Pontus, Galatia, Cappadocia, Asia and Bithynia, who have been chosen according to the foreknowledge of God the Father, through the sanctifying work of the Spirit, to be obedient to Jesus Christ and sprinkled with his blood.*" (1 Peter 1:1b-2a)

So here, we see all three members of the Trinity working in our redemption.

1. The Father's Plan

This passage refers to the foreknowledge of God the Father. His plan has unfolded throughout history and we are his chosen people ("elect exiles" according to 1 Peter 1:1). The Father chose us in Christ before the foundations of the world (see Eph. 1:4).

2. The Spirit's Purification

The Holy Spirit indwells us at the moment of conversion and is a seal of our redemption. Titus 3:5 says, "He saved us, not because of righteous things we had done, but because of his mercy. He saved us through the washing of rebirth and renewal by the Holy Spirit." This purification happens at salvation.

3. The Messiah's Power

The fact that Peter uses the full name *Jesus Christ* is important here. As I did a word study at biblehub.com, it showed that the term Jesus Christ means "the incarnate, the eternal Son of God, the divine Messiah."[1] Now that's a powerful name that has an infinite amount of meaning behind it! Jesus Christ is the long-awaited Messiah who came to earth to save us, and He cleanses us from all of our sins through the power of His blood (His sacrificial death). It is our job to obey the gospel by putting our faith in Jesus Christ. As believers, we have the privilege of walking by faith in our gracious God, and He gives us *peace*. In fact, the apostle mentions **grace and peace** in his opening remarks. In verse 2b, he says, "May grace and peace be multiplied to you." Notice that grace precedes peace. We have been given grace from God, and therefore, we have peace with God and peace in our hearts (and unity with other believers [see 1 Peter 3:8]).

Now that we've covered various aspects of the introductory verses of First Peter, let's read it one more time with fresh eyes and a deeper perspective...

Peter, an apostle of Jesus Christ,

To God's elect, exiles scattered throughout the provinces of Pontus, Galatia, Cappadocia, Asia and Bithynia, *²who have been chosen according to the foreknowledge of God the Father, through the sanctifying work of the Spirit, to be obedient to Jesus Christ and sprinkled with his blood:*

Grace and peace be yours in abundance. (1 Peter 1:1-2)

What a marvelous beginning to a magnificent book of the Bible!

May you experience **peace** as you walk in the **grace** of our Triune God today (and forevermore)!

---

1. *HELPS Word-studies*. Helps Ministries, Inc. 2011. https://biblehub.com/greek/2424.htm

A Glorious Inheritance

26

As I sit in my office today and type these words on my keyboard, my eyes are drawn toward my window where I see a bunch of trees and our church parking lot. The light rain that is falling caused me to think of how much I enjoy the weather here in Missouri.

It is temperate and the winters are not too cold, and there are beautiful sunny days in the spring, summer, and fall. However, I have found that many people complain about the weather quite often where I live in mid-Missouri. If it isn't the heat, they're complaining about the winter storms; if it isn't the storms, they're complaining about the humidity. I have to ask the question: *Why the complaining?* Why can't we just enjoy the weather that is given to us each day? And if today's weather isn't ideal, why not try to enjoy it as best as we can and *look forward* to tomorrow (or a date in the near future) when the weather will be better?

Looking forward to an exciting future can be a healthy practice, and it is definitely a healthy practice of the Christian life. The apostle Peter says that we should look forward to our inheritance in Christ because it is an inheritance that can never perish, spoil or fade. Let's read today's passage...

1 Peter 1:4 says, *"[You have obtained] an inheritance that can never perish, spoil or fade. This inheritance is kept in heaven for you."*

The English Standard Versions puts it this way: *"[You have obtained] an inheritance that is imperishable, undefiled, and unfading, kept in heaven for you."*

The Greek word *kleronomian* means an inheritance (or heritage), and in the Old Testament it describes the gift of the Promised Land that God gave to His chosen people.[1] When this word is used in the New Testament it is viewed in one sense as a possession (in the present), and in another sense as something that we participate in or have a share in in the future.

Think of the word inheritance from a historical and family background. A rich man would have a large estate and as he got to the end of his life, he would leave his inheritance to his children (whom he loved). We have a perfect Father and He loves us with a love more powerful than we can imagine, and we have an inheritance because we are co-heirs with His perfect Son!

As I studied more deeply in First Peter 1:4, I dug up three words that describe our inheritance that I want you to remember.

Undecaying (an inheritance that is imperishable...)

The word that is translated "imperishable" could actually be translated "undecaying."[2] Our inheritance in Christ will never deteriorate! Jesus is the same yesterday, today, and forever! (See Heb. 13:8) The concept of not decaying harkens us back to Peter's sermon on the day of Pentecost. In Acts 2:27b, Peter declares, "You will not let your holy one see decay."

Undefiled (an inheritance that is...undefiled...)

This means that our inheritance is untainted, unstained, and free from contamination.[3] Our inheritance is so perfect and unblemished because it is in Christ. Jesus is free from contamination and He did not sin, even though He was tempted in every way. He is preparing a place for us that is untainted, unstained, and devoid of sin. Thankfully, the Holy Spirit is fashioning us for heaven, and He will make us perfect for heaven at the very end of our earthly life.

Unfading (an inheritance that is... unfading...)

The glory of Jesus Christ will never fade away.[4] We will enjoy our inheritance in Christ forever. Paul speaks of "God's glory displayed in the face of Christ." (2 Cor. 4:6a) In a very real sense, we can begin enjoying our inheritance now because we are in Christ. We have been united with Him through the Holy Spirit because of the perfect substitutionary death of Jesus on our behalf.

The fullness of enjoying our inheritance in Christ will come on the other side of eternity, but I declare to you (brother or sister in Christ) that you should dance in your inheritance today!

———

1. Strong, James. *Strong's Exhaustive Concordance of the Bible*. Abingdon Press, 1890.

2. *NAS Exhaustive Concordance of the Bible with Hebrew-Aramaic and Greek Dictionaries*. The Lockman Foundation, 1998. https://biblehub.com/greek/862a.htm

3. Strong, James. *Strong's Exhaustive Concordance of the Bible*. Abingdon Press, 1890.

4. *NAS Exhaustive Concordance of the Bible with Hebrew-Aramaic and Greek Dictionaries*. The Lockman Foundation, 1998. https://biblehub.com/greek/263.htm

Fellowship Maintained!

27

When I was growing up, I wanted to be like my dad. I was close with both of my parents and my maternal grandparents. They showed me how to live and how to love. We had a lot of fun, too! The memories I have from my childhood are very precious to me, and I benefited from growing up in a highly loving environment.

It is the natural progression for a child to walk in his father's (or mother's) footsteps.

Today's study will be in the Book of First John, and the topic is walking in the light. John states that God is light, and therefore, his children must *walk in the light.*

John also uses the word fellowship twice in our passage. So, we will see that maintaining fellowship is a key to walking in the light. As we read today's passage, make sure to keep an eye out for the word "fellowship."

John 1:5-10 *This is the message we have heard from him and declare to you: God is light; in him there is no darkness at all. ⁶ If we claim to have fellowship with him and yet walk in the darkness, we lie and do not live out the truth. ⁷ But if we walk in the light, as he is in the light, we have fellowship with one another, and the blood of Jesus, his Son, purifies us from all sin. ⁸ If we claim to be without sin, we deceive ourselves and the truth is not in us. ⁹ If we confess our sins, he is faithful and just and will forgive us our sins and purify us from all unrighteousness. ¹⁰ If we claim we have not sinned, we make him out to be a liar and his word is not in us.*

Did you see our "key word" there?

We have **fellowship** with the Father and His Son because we have been cleansed by the blood of Jesus. This leads to us having **fellowship** with one another. (v.7)

Jesus paid the price as a perfect sin offering as our substitute, satisfying the wrath of the Father. As we walk out our Christian life, we can have consistent fellowship with God and one another if we walk in God's light and regularly turn away from sin through confession. Jesus is faithful and just to forgive our sins and cleanse us from all unrighteousness! (v. 9) This is a profound truth that needs to be preached and lived out!

We also see in verse 9 that regular confession of sin (with repentance) maintains our closeness with God.

Children in healthy families have (and maintain) fellowship with their father and mother. Children also should do their best to maintain fellowship with their siblings.

It is the same with us as Christians; maintaining fellowship is key. We maintain fellowship with our Father through confession of sin and walking in His light. We keep fellowship with our Christian brothers and sisters by walking in the light together.

Confessing your sin to a fellow Christian is helpful because it gets the sin out in the light. Also, many congregations have a time of corporate confession each Sunday as they endeavor to walk in the light together.

The purpose of all of these practices is to help believers stay close to God and receive His fresh cleansing on a consistent basis. What a joy it is to walk in the light and have fellowship with our Lord! It definitely helps keep the conscience clear.

The two main application points that I see emerging from this passage are...

1. Know God and walk in His light (v. 5-7)

2. Regularly confess your sins and receive Christ's cleansing (v. 8-10)

As you finish this devotional reading and go about your day, remember the main idea of passage, which is this: We can have fellowship with God and one another if we walk in God's light and regularly turn away from sin through confession.

Ages and Stages

28

Have you ever met a middle-age person who acted like a child?

Or, conversely... have you ever met a teenager who was incredibly mature for their age?

In today's passage (1 John 2:12-13a), we are going to read about *spiritual age*...

12 I am writing to you, dear children,
  because your sins have been forgiven on account of His name.
13 I am writing to you, fathers,
  because you know Him who is from the beginning.
I am writing to you, young men,
  because you have overcome the evil one.

John is writing to believers to encourage them in their faith. He uses the term "dear children" seven times in the Book of First John, and when he uses the term he seems to be referring to all Christians because they are all children of God. Take First John 2:1 for example, John says, "My dear children, I write this to you so that you will not sin. But if anybody does sin, we have an advocate with the Father—Jesus Christ, the Righteous One."

So, when John tells all Christians that their "sins have been forgiven on account of His name." we should shout for joy! The phrase literally means that all of our sins have been sent away[1] on the authority of the Name of Jesus on account of what He did for us!

After John lays the foundation of the *forgiven status* of all Christians, he delves into two spiritual age categories. He begins with the *fathers*... "I am writing to you, fathers, because you know Him who is from the beginning."

Spiritual fathers and mothers have walked with God for a significant length of time. They know Christ and the power of His resurrection. Their close relationship with God is evidenced by the way they live their life, and they are an example to others. Spiritual parents seek to help others come to Christ *and* grow in Christ.

John then moves to the *young men*. He states, "I am writing to you, young men, because you have overcome the evil one."

As John encourages young people in the faith, he emphasizes that they are victorious over Satan's power. The Greek word for *overcome* that John uses carries the idea of conquering, prevailing, and emerging victorious.[2] Young people in the faith, due to the fact that they are in Christ, have overcome the evil one! This is no small thing! Satan has been defeated and these young people are walking in victory.

Believers who are 'younger in the faith' need to learn from their spiritual fathers and mothers. Young people benefit greatly when they come under the leadership (mentorship) of a spiritual parent.

I have personally experienced how great it can be when a spiritual parent gently comes alongside a younger believer and helps them mature in the faith. Whether I was the person being mentored or the person doing the mentoring, the relationship that was built was meaningful and helpful.

Isn't it beautiful how these two age groups can work together!

As we wrap up today, I will loop back to the concept that I mentioned in the introduction. Spiritual age is the term I want to highlight. Spiritual age often correlates with physical age, but it *does not always* correlate with physical age. For example, a 48 year-old man who has been walking with God for many years may become a mentor to a 58 year-old man who is a newer believer.

The typical pattern is that the older person mentors the younger person, but it is worth noting that that is not always the case.

It is a sweet environment when seasoned believers are mentoring younger believers! You can pray that this environment is cultivated in your church and in your city!

Oh, the wonder and beauty of the gospel! That we have been forgiven on account of His Name! May we deepen our walk with Christ and help others move forward with Him (all the days of our lives)!

———

1. Strong, James. *Strong's Exhaustive Concordance of the Bible.* Abingdon Press, 1890. https://biblehub.com/greek/863.htm

2. Strong, James. *Strong's Exhaustive Concordance of the Bible.* Abingdon Press, 1890. https://biblehub.com/greek/3528.htm

Chapter 5:
Follow God's Guidance!

(7 Devotional Readings)

Young and Free

29

Being a young person in today's world is *far from easy*. I work with youth and young adults at a church in mid-Missouri, and it is becoming abundantly apparent that the challenges facing our young people are increasing.

The fact that information is so readily available on a young person's phone is both a blessing and a curse. I have noticed that a higher percentage of young people struggle to set limits on how much they use their phone, as compared to people who are middle-age or older.

So, young people need to be properly equipped and effectively mobilized if they are going to succeed in today's world. There is a young man (Eli) in my youth group that has remained connected with his family and our church. He is a positive example to the younger students in the youth group. He shows respect to his parents and his siblings. Eli demonstrates his work ethic at his part-time job and as a leader on his wrestling team.

There are many other positive examples of thriving young people in my youth group and in our community. However, as I observe and interact with young people in mid-Missouri, I also see many who are struggling to gain their footing and find their purpose. One youth I spoke with yesterday said that he wanted to find his purpose in life. I explained to him that he needs to find his purpose in God and then allow the Lord to direct him on his calling in life.

As I was looking in God's Word today, I dug up *3 golden nuggets for youth*.

If you have a young person in your life that you are trying to encourage (or if you are a young person), these are words that will speak into your situation.

1. Youth should pursue... a **pure pathway**.

"How can a young person stay on the path of purity? By living according to your word." (Psalm 119:9)

This verse clearly articulates that young people need to be in God's Word and strive to live according to it. This is the only way to stay on the path of purity. There is so much junk out there that is bombarding our youth. We need to come alongside them and help them pursue the path of purity. It's not an easy path and it's not a popular path, but it's a path that brings the joy of God.

2. Youth should pursue... **parental involvement**.

"Listen, my son, to your father's instruction and do not forsake your mother's teaching. They are a garland to grace your head and a chain to adorn your neck." (Proverbs 1:8-9)

Many young people try to avoid the instruction that their parents are trying to provide. However, this verse shows us that youth shouldn't just tolerate their parents' involvement, they should lean into their parents' guidance. The wisdom that young people learn from their parents should be cherished and followed with joy. Let's not squander these opportunities! Let's make sure these connections take place!

3. Youth should pursue... the **plans of the Lord**.

"'For I know the plans I have for you,' declares the Lord, 'plans to prosper you and not to harm you, plans to give you hope and a future.'" (Jeremiah 29:11)

Sometimes, young people spend a lot of time planning where they're going to go and what they're going to do, and they forget (neglect) to ask God what their plan should be. It is vital to seek wisdom and to involve God in your planning process. Don't make the mistake of doing all the planning yourself and then asking God to bless it. God's plans are good and they will give you hope and a future.

Jeremiah 29:11 shows us that you will prosper if you follow God's plan for your life. It may not be prosperity in the world's eyes, but it will be prosperity in God's eyes. Young people can have joy and peace as they navigate through life, and they will honor God as they pursue His plan for their life.

As we wrap up, think of a young person in your life that you need to call up and encourage this week. I bet they will be glad to hear from you.

We need to make *relational* **re**connection. The young person will benefit from the advice and support given by the mentor, and the mentor will receive joy and encouragement as well. Let's help our young people pursue a pure pathway and remain *connected* with their parents, so that they will *thrive* and accomplish the plan that God has for their life.

Vibrancy

30

I have a friend named Jake who lives in northeastern Minnesota in the town of Grand Marais (on the shore of Lake Superior). In this beautiful little tourist town, they have seven months of winter and five months of bad sledding!

Jake and I met at a Youth Minister's Conference in Florida. The conference was designed for youth leaders and their spouses to have a weekend of refreshment and rejuvenation.

Jake and his wife lead the youth group at Grand Marais Evangelical Free Church. Jake is caring and he is a good listener. He is a man of prayer. He and I developed a close friendship over the last year and half. I have felt a lot of support from him whenever I need wise counsel on a situation.

I simply call or text Jake, and we set up a time to talk. I am able to share what is going on in my life, and he is excellent at giving a timely word that helps me tackle the situation I'm dealing with. What's even greater than his solid advice is his heart. He texted me after one of our phone conversations to let me know that he's praying for me. He checked in a few days later to ask me how my situation panned out, *and to let me know that he was praying.* **For this I am very thankful.**

I've been reading sections of 2 Thessalonians lately, and I came across a verse today that encapsulates how Jake lives out his faith. It's 2 Thessalonians 1:12.

The verse says, *"We pray this so that the name of our Lord Jesus may be glorified in you, and you in Him, according to the grace of our God and the Lord Jesus Christ."*

There are three keys to vibrancy in our walk with God that are shown in this verse.

1. Prayer

The verse begins with two important words, "We pray." Personal prayer is essential, but group prayer brings even more power! Jesus said, "If two of you on earth agree about anything they ask for, it will be done for them by my Father in heaven." (Matt. 18:19) Make sure you make time for prayer. Even praying before a meal or at bedtime is no small thing!

2. Focusing on the Lord's glory

Our theme verse expresses the importance of "the name of our Lord Jesus" being glorified. God is so good! We should praise Him for how awesome He is! He is so loving and He is so holy, and He does all things for His glory. We are doing what we were meant to do as humans when we bask in the awesomeness of His glory.

3. God's grace

God's grace is shown to us in so many ways, even in the little things in life. Supremely, His grace is shown to us in what Jesus did for us in redemption. The fact that He took on flesh, lived a perfect life, and bore *all* of our sins on the cross is a mighty act of love and grace. His grace flows to us, and we should allow it to flow through us. We should thank Him regularly for His bountiful grace.

I am grateful to have a friend like Jake who demonstrates these three key aspects in his life on a daily basis. I look forward to gleaning more nuggets of wisdom from my buddy from northeastern MN (I am going to call him today!). Most of all, I look forward to growing in vibrancy in my walk with the Lord as I continue to trek forward with fellow believers [like Jake] by my side.

I hope that you will build your web of encouragement with supportive people in your life. They will speak into your life, and you will speak into theirs.

As you give encouragement and receive encouragement, let the three keys we talked about today shine through. *Spend time in prayer, focus on the Lord's glory, and trust in God's grace.*

Extreme Life Makeover

31

Over the years, we have all seen home improvement shows that take a subpar house and make it into a beautifully restored masterpiece. It is quite a sight at the end of the show when they do the **big reveal**. Whether it's *Fixer Upper, Property Brothers,* or *Love It or List It,* the effect is the same; people love seeing a "dream home" arise out of a dilapidated habitation.

Viewers "journey" with the prospective home buyers in search of a living situation that will meet all their preferences (and then some). Oftentimes, the designers will make decisions to move walls and gut kitchens in order to provide an open concept with better flooring and cabinetry. It is fun to watch the whole process unfold as they make choices about what features will be on display in their new house. However, *the last time slot* of the show is the real payoff. The *big reveal* is so compelling that they always have a commercial break before it because they know you'll stay tuned to see the final product.

As I think about how we are glued to the TV screen for these repetitive (yet intriguing) shows on *HGTV*, it makes me think about how God wants to provide major restoration to all the areas of my life. *He wants that for your life, too.* Instead of Extreme Home Makeover, this is **Extreme Life Makeover**. The transformation that God wants to do through His Spirit's presence and work in our lives is never finished (but hopefully we can see significant progress).

What steps of transformation have occurred in your life recently? What steps of transformation do you believe God wants to do in your life in the near future? How can you cooperate with Him?

Jesus died for our sins so that we would be saved *and* sanctified. Therefore, we should pursue our sanctification process with joy and fervor. Yes, it does involve rooting out sin and old patterns that need to be thrown to the wayside. We do probably need to gut a few areas of our lives, but keep in mind that God has something better in store for you. It will be different and may not be what you expected. Most of us struggle with change, so as you ask God to do a transformative work in your life, you should also ask him to help you be more adjustable to changes in your life.

Remember the sledge hammers from the home improvement shows? Perhaps one of the areas of your life needs a sledge hammer (i.e., immediate removal; radical amputation). However, in much of my experience with people and in my own life, God comes into our "home" with His gentle hands and kindly works with us to help us let go of things.

Sometimes the things we need to let go of are not necessarily bad things. Nevertheless, it is beneficial to let go of them because God has something better in store for us.

So, what will you do in response to reading this today?

First off, I hope you will have peace because you know that God is on your side and that He will take care of you.

And lastly, I want you to arise each day with excitement *and* with an expectation that God is going to continue to transform your life. It won't be easy. And He is going to use the "sandpaper" of His Holy Spirit to round off the rough edges of your life.

The whole process will be worth it because you will draw nearer to God and become more like Christ. You will be thankful for the changes that God brings about in your life because it will bring glory to Him and be an example to others.

But remember, you need to cooperate with Him. That's why Ephesians 5:14b says, "Wake up, sleeper, and rise from the dead, and Christ will shine on you." Notice how this verse shows us that we need to **arise**. And then the logical next step is that we need to make the changes that God wants us to make as Christ shines His light on us.

Isaiah 60:1 declares, "Arise, shine, for your light has come, and the glory of the Lord rises upon you."

So, as you go about your life, be on the lookout for God's activity. May you arise and experience a season of transformation! And may God restore all the "rooms" of your life so that you display His glory and shine like a beautiful masterpiece.

ONE

32

There is a book of the Bible that has become one of my favorite places to read in God's Word. This New Testament epistle was also mentioned by my sister as one of her favorites. The book I am referring to is Ephesians.

For my parents' wedding, there were two verses in Ephesians that were the theme verses at their ceremony, and there are two verses in that same book that were the theme verses for my wedding with Gracie.

I guess you could say that it's a book of the Bible that speaks strongly to my entire family.

Nestled between my parents' theme verse (Eph. 3:20-21) and Gracie and my theme verse (Eph. 5:1-2) is a glorious chapter of the Bible. The chapter that I am referring to is obviously Ephesians 4, and it has spoken strongly to me on countless occasions. This section of the Bible is one of my "playgrounds" in Scripture.

Allow me to share a few verses from Ephesians 4 with you. This is Ephesians 4:4-6.

There is one body and one Spirit, just as you were called to one hope when you were called; one Lord, one faith, one baptism; one God and Father of all, who is over all and through all and in all.

Paul is writing to the Church in Ephesus and he is imploring them to stay unified in Christ through the power of the Holy Spirit. He uses the word "one" to make his point. He actually says the word "one" seven times to emphatically drive home his point. It's like he's shouting to us from a mountaintop saying, "One, one, one!!"

But what does 'being one' look like? Well, as I've studied this passage, I've seen that the concept of **one** is fleshed out in the first half of this chapter (Eph 4:1-16). Paul wants unification for these believers. To be 'one' is to be unified, and Paul has three areas of unity that he wants these believers to walk in.

1. Unity with Christ because He has called us

Eph. 4:1, *"As a prisoner for the Lord, then, I urge you to live a life worthy of the calling you have received."*

2. Unity in our interactions

Eph 4:2, *"Be completely humble and gentle; be patient, bearing with one another in love."*

3. Unity under our Christian leaders

Eph. 4:11-13, *"So Christ himself gave the apostles, the prophets, the evangelists, the pastors and teachers, to equip his people for works of service, so that the body of Christ may be built up until we all reach unity in the faith and in the knowledge of the Son of God and become mature, attaining to the whole measure of the fullness of Christ."*

These are important concepts that the apostle Paul lays out clearly in Ephesians 4. I can't think of three concepts that are more crucial than these. I will even highlight point #2 (unity in our interactions) because our communication with people is so important. And whether it's interacting in a marriage, a family, at church, or in the community, when it's done in love, that's what counts. The verse that I referenced is a powerful one. It's Ephesians 4:2 and it says, "With all humility and gentleness, with patience, showing tolerance for one another in love."

Wow! What a massive statement! What a game-plan for living! If all marriages would follow this verse, marriage problems would go down to virtually nothing. Church conflict would disappear! Families would stay together and actually enjoy time together on a daily basis!

I will wrap up this installment by mentioning how thankful I am for my wife. She is truly a blessing to me and our children. At the time of this writing, we are preparing to celebrate our 10-year anniversary. We tied the knot on August 27, 2011. Extended family members came from all over the Midwest to be at our wedding, and we are thankful that they could witness our commitment to be **one**.

As we walk out our calling and follow our Christian leaders, we will live life the way it was meant to be lived. We will show the love of God in all of our interactions, consistently looking for a way to build others up.

When believers are walking in unity it is incredibly sweet, and God wants us to be vigilant to maintain unity. (See Eph. 4:3)

May you experience the unity that only God can provide with the fellow believers in your life. Amen. [So be it.]

Relationships!

33

A couple of years ago, a small group Bible study formed among some young families at our church. My wife and I have the privilege of being part of this wonderful group of believers. We recently went through the Book of Ephesians, chapter by chapter.

I enjoyed it thoroughly! One of the highlights of this group is the supplemental resource that we used to help us understand some deeper aspects of Ephesians. The book is called "Sit, Walk, Stand" and it's by Watchman Nee.

In Paul's letter to the Ephesians, he covers many rich doctrines in six robust chapters that are loaded with deep biblical principles. There is a transition that takes place as the book moves from chapter three to chapter four. The last word of chapter three is "amen," and the first word of chapter four is "therefore." These transition words are key markers that the second three chapters will build on the foundation that was laid in the first three chapters.

I was able to gather some insight from Nee's book about this hinge point in Ephesians. Nee writes, "Paul proceeds, in the light of our heavenly calling, to challenge us upon the whole field of our relationships."[1]

The first three chapters of Ephesians are critical because believers are instructed to reckon that they have been "saved by grace through faith" and that they are part of a redeemed fellowship (i.e. the Body of Christ). Nee affirms, "The Body of Christ, the fellowship of Christian believers, is [a] great theme of Ephesians."[2]

There are four verses in the latter part of Ephesians 4 that give us some specific guidance on how we should treat other people.

These verses were written to the members of the Church at Ephesus some 1,950 years ago, but they can be applied to our lives.

Let's read the passage.

Ephesians 4:25-28 says, "*Therefore, having put away falsehood, let each one of you speak the truth with his neighbor, for we are members one of another. Be angry and do not sin; do not let the sun go down on your anger, and give no opportunity to the devil. Let the thief no longer steal, but rather let him labor, doing honest work with his own hands, so that he may have something to share with anyone in need.*"

I see three key points that can be gleaned from these verses.

1. Speak the truth to one another.

It is crucial that we stay away from falsehood and speak the truth in love to each other.

2. Subdue your anger with God's help.

Unaddressed anger will cause you to become bitter. Ask God to help you deal with your anger in a healthy way.

3. Share with others from the fruits of your labor.

Honest work and open hands will be a blessing to your community. Share with your neighbors and give a hand to those in need.

Relationships are a HUGE aspect of our lives. God made us as relational beings. The most important relationship we can have is with God because of what Jesus did for us on the Cross. As we walk with Christ, *we love others because we have been shown such great love from God.* (See 1 John 4:10, 19)

I think my friend Jake Patten captured this sentiment very well so I'll let him have the final word. He wrote, "Praise the Lord Jesus for His indescribable gift of righteousness by His blood on our behalf! May we walk out this righteousness to His glory, today and forever."

---

1. Nee, Watchman. *Sit, Walk, Stand.* Carol Stream, Ill: Tyndale House Publishers, 1977.
2. Ibid.

All Saints Eve Party

34

There is a wonderful gospel-preaching church called North Heights on the north side of the Twin Cities. I had the privilege of attending this church for the first eight years of my life. The church is led by a team of great pastors and it has two campuses; one in Arden Hills (MN) and another in Roseville (MN). There was always a fabulous event on the last day of October every year. It was the **All Saints Eve Party**.

The party took a lot of planning, and when it was at its peak there were 1,000 kids who came and 500 volunteers who served. *There were so many people that they had to utilize both campuses!* Holding an event like this requires a point-person who has exceptional communication skills and high organizational aptitude.

This is where my ***aunt Luann*** enters the picture. She was the leader of the All Saints Eve Party for ***many*** years, and she did her job with gusto! There was a meal, bouncy houses, entertainment, and a lot of **free candy and rich fellowship**.

I remember going to this incredibly fun event each year on October 31. It was a wonderful substitute for Halloween, which can be a dark holiday, especially in big cities. The kids enjoyed a loving environment that was filled with joy and laughter. Parents were able to socialize and connect during this "family-oriented" extravaganza at North Heights. Costumes were optional and the uplifting atmosphere was devoid of the darker images that Halloween often celebrates. What a blessing! What a great opportunity for fellowship and outreach!

Aunt Luann designed the All Saints Eve Party to focus on the *light* and not the darkness.

Similarly, it is important for us in our lives to focus on the light of our Lord and not on the darkness. When we walk in God's truth, dark things are exposed for what they really are... trash.

Ephesians 5:8-10 is an excellent passage that can help us see with proper vision. Let's read these three powerful verses.

For you were once darkness, but now you are light in the Lord. Live as children of light (for the fruit of the light consists in all goodness, righteousness and truth) and find out what pleases the Lord. (Eph. 5:8-10)

Let's take a moment to discern what the main point of this passage is and see if we can glean any application points.

<u>Main point</u>: We are instructed to reckon ourselves as children of light and avoid the darkness as we walk in ways that are honoring to God.

<u>Application</u>: As we face daily decisions in our *faith walk*, we should ask ourselves the following questions before partaking in any given activity.

1. Is it good?

2. Is it right?

3. Is it true?

4. Is it pleasing to the Lord?

The first three questions are based off of Ephesians 5:9... "for the fruit of the light consists in all goodness, righteousness and truth. And the fourth question is based off of verse 10, which says, "And find out what pleases the Lord."

If we ask ourselves these four essential questions (and answer them biblically), we will keep ourselves from a lot of poor decisions and sinful patterns. There are many "dark" activities that take place in our culture, and it's not just during late October each year. We need to be on guard! We need to stay in the light and not stray into the darkness.

That's why God gives us the light of His Word. I bought a new flashlight recently, and I've already used it in my backyard to illuminate things as I walk around in the evening.

We need to use God's Word like a flashlight as we try to stay on His path in the midst of our culture that is filled with darkness.

Psalm 119:105, "Your word is a lamp for my feet, a light on my path."

As we wrap up, I will mention *All Saints Day* again. It is a "holiday" that occurs every year on November 1, and it's a day to honor our Christian brothers and sisters that have gone on to be with the Lord. I believe that this "cloud of witnesses" is cheering us on to move forward in God's light and steer clear of the darkness. (See Hebrews 12:1)

May we all "walk as children of light" and follow the Lord as we rely on His Word to light our pathway!

Shaken or Solid

35

I went to the Firley YMCA recently in Jefferson City (MO), and I met a nice man named Jordan. When I walked into the workout center, Jordan was the only one exercising in the middle area, which consists of ellipticals and stationary bikes. He was working up a good sweat and burning off the holiday calories.

As Jordan was stepping off his elliptical, I was beginning my workout on the *ArcTrainer* and he struck up a conversation with me.

We delved into an encouraging conversation about what's going in his life. I enjoyed hearing about his family and his work-life. He told me that he works out at the Y every day for an hour. He also told me that he lives in an apartment very close to the Y and that he works at a gas station that is down the street from the Y.

I found his traveling schedule to be pretty to be very **efficient**. Your apartment, your job, and your gym all within short walking distance. Wow! He mentioned that he saves a lot of money on gas. *I'd say so!!*

He indicated that exercising each day helps him keep a healthy body and a healthy mind.

He told me that he had lost 27 pounds by exercising every day and taking an affordable health shake. I congratulated him, and he told me that he is going to continue to stay on his health track. He religiously takes the health powder and shakes it up in his shaker bottle on a daily basis. He even showed me the bottle that he uses and I could tell that he is committed to his process.

I took a moment to ponder the picture lessons that were being shown to me at that moment. In my mind, the shaker bottle represented how people were shaken up in 2020 due to the pandemic. Jordan represented someone who is sticking to a solid process, and that is helping him feel more solid.

It really hit me. People are either **shaken or solid**. They are either going to find solid ground or suffer on shaky ground.

I could easily tie in the story that Jesus tells in Matthew 7 about the wise man building his house on the rock and the foolish man building his house on the sand. However, the Scripture that is on my mind today (that guided me to use these illustrations with Jordan) is Ephesians 6:12-14a. This verse is about the first piece of armor in the armor of God passage, *the belt of truth*.

The Bible says that we are in a battle and that the enemy is trying to take us out. Ephesians 6:12 says, "For our struggle is not against flesh and blood, but against the rulers, against the authorities, against the powers of this dark world and against the spiritual forces of evil in the heavenly realms."

We are in a battle! The enemy wants to take us down, and he will use anything to discourage us, even a pandemic or politics.

Paul instructs us to stand firm and to put on the armor of God in Ephesians 6:13.

"Therefore put on the full armor of God, so that when the day of evil comes, you may be able to stand your ground, and after you have done everything, to stand."

Then we arrive at our theme verse for the day, Ephesians 6:14a. Paul directs, "Stand firm then, with the belt of truth buckled around your waist."

We need to be properly equipped because we live in a fallen world and the enemy wants to throw lies at us. We need to be girded with truth.

God wants us to be truth-tellers. He gives us His Spirit, and Jesus takes up residence in our hearts by faith. (See Eph. 3:16)

In John 14:6, Jesus states that he is "the truth." We gird ourselves with Christ, who is the truth! He is the belt that we should put on every day!

We learn more about His truth by reading his Word on a consistent basis. It is important for us to interact with the truth of God's Word. Sitting under good Bible teaching at a Christ-centered church is a **must** if you want to grow in your walk with God over the long haul.

The main lesson today is that we can be solid, instead of shaken, even during tough times.

Put on Christ, who is the truth.

He will help us...

1. *Walk* in truth.

2. *Tell* the truth.

3. *Defend* with truth.

Chapter 6:
<u>Thank the Lord!</u>

(7 Devotional Readings)

One-Liners

36

When people are hanging out with friends or watching comedic entertainment, it is a healthy sign when you hear laughter. Oftentimes, it's a funny story or a "one-liner" that can really get people busting their gut.

The *one-liner* is a helpful item in the toolbox of a person with a strong sense of humor. The fact that it is "short and sweet" enhances the effectiveness of the line. When delivered well, the line can not only create humor in the moment but it can stick with the person who heard it as a "little lesson" if there is a nugget of truth in the one-liner.

The apostle Paul used some incredible one-liners near the end of First Thessalonians. He had a knack for using short pithy statements to implore believers to live out their faith, and this passage takes the cake. Let's read the concise passage.

1 Thessalonians 5:16-18, *"Rejoice always, pray continually, give thanks in all circumstances; for this is God's will for you in Christ Jesus."*

These three powerful nudges that Paul gave to the Thessalonians were intended to help them live out God's will for their lives.

Don't gloss over the last part of the passage. Paul strongly declares that "this is God's will for you in Christ Jesus." The apostle is essentially saying that the previous three affirmations are massively important for believers if they are going to walk in God's will. Wow! We don't want to miss this!

Paul's encouraging words to the Thessalonians are words that can be directly applied to our lives as we endeavor to walk in God's ways.

So, let's list out the three "quick hits" as a *trio of signposts* as a way for our eyes and mind to digest them again.

1. Rejoice always (v. 16)

2. Pray continually (v. 17)

3. Give thanks in all circumstances (v. 18a)

These are three keys to spiritual growth. If we consistently rejoice, pray continually, and cultivate thankfulness, we will grow in the Lord.

It makes sense that these three things would be indispensable ingredients for our spiritual life because Jesus exemplified all three of these actions. His joy was in doing the work of His Father, and we see that throughout his earthly ministry. Prayer was a way of life for Jesus as He had ongoing communication with His Father. He even stepped away from His disciples for extended times of prayer. In addition, we see Jesus giving thanks to the Father for His wisdom and love.

What a marvelous Savior we have in Jesus! He is our example!

You will grow in your spiritual walk and become more like Christ if you do the three things mentioned in our passage today. *Rejoice always, pray continually, and give thanks in all circumstances; for this is God's will for you in Christ Jesus.*

Look Up!

37

There is a **great verse** in the Psalms that I will highlight today. This verse is actually the last verse of both Psalm 42 *AND* 43.

Psalm 42:11 *"Why, my soul, are you downcast? Why so disturbed within me? Put your hope in God, for I will yet praise Him, my Savior and my God."*

Psalm 43:5 *"Why, my soul, are you downcast? Why so disturbed within me? Put your hope in God, for I will yet praise Him, my Savior and my God."*

I find this verse to be so encouraging because it is realistic, heart-wrenching, and honest. The psalmist looks to God even in the midst of his angst.

Maybe you've done the same thing in the past when you've gone through hard times. You called out to God when you were at your lowest, and He answered your prayer and provided you with comfort and strength. When trouble comes, it is absolutely essential to find our hope in Him.

For many of us, we can look back and say that there have been sweet seasons of growth when the waves have been calm and God has taught us wonderful things. However, the winds and torrents always eventually come, and the big question is... where will we turn to when times get tough?

The psalmist gives us a wonderful example.

At the top of this page, I wrote out both Psalm 42:11 and 43:5 to prove to you that they are both written in the exact same way. A text note in my Bible says that "in many Hebrew manuscripts Psalms 42 and 43 constitute one psalm." This information helps us understand that these psalms go together.

Let the words of this psalm bring you hope and encouragement, and let it provide an example for you to follow during difficult seasons and "down days" in your life.

Psalm 42:11 and 43:5 *"Why, my soul, are you downcast? Why so disturbed within me? Put your hope in God, for I will yet praise Him, my Savior and my God."*

The psalmist shows us the way to be honest with our emotions, deal with reality, look to God, and praise Him for being our Savior.

If you are down, **don't stay there!** God can lift you up! Look to Him. Put your hope in Him and lift your voice in praise.

Let's look at the sections of this phenomenal verse.

1. Admit your sadness to God in the midst of your situation.

"Why, my soul, are you downcast? Why so disturbed within me?" (Psalm 42:11a)

Go to God in the midst of your pain. Don't try to wait until your pain is over. He is there for you. He wants you to come to Him, and He is not surprised by your sadness or your situation.

2. Praise the Lord in the midst of your situation.

"Put your hope in God, for I will yet praise Him, my Savior and my God." (Psalm 42:11b)

It is a wonderful thing when you lift your heart to the Lord and praise Him even as you are in your struggle. There is great joy in that. There is great comfort that happens and, most importantly, God is glorified. He is our Savior and He is our God. He deserves our praise, no matter our situation.

You will find that these verses that are found in the 42nd and 43rd Psalm are a key to not only this difficult season but to our entire lives. We need to look to God when we feel downcast and disturbed. When we put our hope in God and say, "I will yet praise Him," His light will shine on our faces in a fresh way. I love how he uses the word "yet." *I will YET praise Him.* (emphasis added)

Psalm 42:11 and 43:5 are the last verses of Psalm 42 and 43, respectively. Both verses are a wonderful capstone to these "tandem psalms." I even found this same exact verse in the middle of Psalm 42. That's right! It's found in a third place in these psalms (42:5)!! I will let the words of the psalmist end our devotional today. Put your hope in the Lord and praise Him in the midst of any difficulties you are facing.

Psalm 42:5 *"Why, my soul, are you downcast? Why so disturbed within me? Put your hope in God, for I will yet praise Him, my Savior and my God."*

Thankful for Christ

38

One of the ladies who goes to Living Hope Church is named Kay. She has lived in Jefferson City for a long time and she has told me many stories from her time in this community. Kay is 93 years old and she has become my friend. She loves it when people stop by her house for a visit.

Phone calls from her family and friends are appreciated by Kay, especially during the winter months. She has mentioned several times that the visits and the phone calls have been such a big help to her because she often feels **lonely**.

I think a lot of people feel lonely on a regular basis, and it's important for all of us to make the extra effort by picking up the phone or stopping by someone's house to chat.

A simple phone call (a.k.a. "*encouragement call*") is a phenomenal tool that we have in our *toolbox,* and we should be using that tool frequently. Just think, there may be people in your life who are feeling down and a phone call from you could be the vehicle that God uses to lift them up.

Reaching out to people through these simple means is important because it keeps us moving toward each other instead of away from each other.

At Christmas, we celebrate the fact that God moved toward us by sending His Son. Jesus **came** to us. That is powerful. *He came to us and for us.*

Jesus broke into the world on a Christmas Eve some 2,000 years ago when He was born to a virgin.

John 1:14 says, "The Word became flesh and made his dwelling among us. We have seen his glory, the glory of the one and only Son, who came from the Father, full of grace and truth."

This foundational verse in the Gospel of John lays out three key aspects of Jesus coming to us.

1. Jesus took on a human body.

"The Word became flesh and made his dwelling among us." (v. 14a)

2. Jesus showed us His glory.

"We have seen his glory, the glory of the one and only Son, who came from the Father,..." (v. 14b)

3. Jesus showed us how to live in His grace and truth.

"...full of grace and truth." (v. 14c)

He came for us and it is truly glorious that He left His throne in heaven to live in a body on earth. He ultimately came to die in our place.

We should be extremely thankful for this. The gospel is so powerful because it shows us How awesome God is. Jesus paid the full ransom for our sin so that we can live forever with God.

Since Jesus came for us in love, we should move toward other people in love too. We have such a great example in our Lord. What a wonderful Savior!

Jesus shows us the glory of God and He instructs us through His Word on how we should live in His grace and truth.

We should thank the Lord regularly for the fact that He took on a human body to pay for our sins.

Express your thankfulness to the Lord and follow God's pathway. Make a few *encouragement calls* today because as you move toward others, you are following the way of Christ.

In the Father's House

39

There is a man who goes to my church whose name is Matt. He is a *family man* who shows a lot of care for the people in his life. Matt and his wife (Carrie) spend a lot of time with two women in their extended family: Cathy and Mary.

Matt provides these ladies with encouragement on a regular basis. *I am also one of the benefactors of Matt's encouragement.* He always has a kind word to share with me and he keeps a positive disposition. My conversations with him are easy-flowing and we have a true respect for one another.

Matt is one of the people on our Children's Church teaching team. We have a rotation of several teachers, and he teaches the children once per month. He recently taught on the only passage in the Bible that depicts Jesus as a twelve year-old boy. It's a fascinating passage.

Let's read Luke 2:41-48.

Every year Jesus' parents went to Jerusalem for the Festival of the Passover. When he was twelve years old, they went up to the festival, according to the custom. After the festival was over, while his parents were returning home, the boy Jesus stayed behind in Jerusalem, but they were unaware of it. Thinking he was in their company, they traveled on for a day. Then they began looking for him among their relatives and friends. When they did not find him, they went back to Jerusalem to look for him. After three days they found him in the temple courts, sitting among the teachers, listening to them and asking them questions. Everyone who heard him was amazed at his understanding and his answers. When his parents saw him, they were astonished. His mother said to him, "Son, why have you treated us like this? Your father and I have been anxiously searching for you."

In this narrative (as with many other narratives), there is a problem that eventually arises and then a resolution that takes place at the end.

Let's set the scene and then look at the rising action, climax, and resolution.

The scene is set. Jesus is twelve years old, and they are taking their annual family trip to Jerusalem for the Passover Festival. *"Every year Jesus' parents went to Jerusalem for the Festival of the Passover."* (v. 41)

1. A problem occurs. Joseph and Mary cannot find their son in the large caravan of people as they were traveling away from Jerusalem. They need to find the boy. *"When they did not find him, they went back to Jerusalem to look for him."* (v. 45)

2. The climactic discovery and conversation. Joseph and Mary find their son in the temple, reasoning with the teachers. They are upset, but Jesus gently corrects them when He says, *"Why were you searching for me? Didn't you know I had to be in my Father's house?"* (v. 49) His parents did not understand Jesus' statement about how he needed to be in his "Father's house." (See v. 50)

3. A Higher Resolution. Jesus demonstrates His heart for His heavenly Father, and He continues to show respect and love to His parents. As He grows in stature and wisdom, He is preparing for His earthly ministry. Mary remembers and treasures this momentous event at the temple. *"Then he went down to Nazareth with them and was obedient to them. But his mother treasured all these things in her heart. And Jesus grew in wisdom and stature, and in favor with God and man."* (v. 51-52)

So, what is the main idea of the passage?

<u>Main idea</u>: The boy Jesus shows His heart for His Father's business by staying in the temple to reason with the teachers, and His parents observe His growth and obedience.

There are a few basic application points that we glean from this passage, and we will take one from each section of the text.

1. Practice regular worship like Jesus did.

2. Obey the Father, emulating how Jesus obeyed the Father.

3. Increase in wisdom and in favor with God and people.

God will bless us as we endeavor to cultivate these important pillars in our lives. And we will be a *big encouragement* to others as we spur our brothers and sisters on in their walk with the Lord.

Anchor Down!

40

I have enjoyed boating with various members of my family throughout the years. I recall pontooning on Lake Dillon in Colorado in 2015 and boating with my cousins during the summer months in Minnesota in the late 90's and early 2000's. These are fond memories, and the list goes on. There was a Christian camp called Camp Lebanon where we did all different kinds of boating. If it was a paddleboat, a canoe, a kayak, or a pontoon, we did it!

Many folks I know (myself included) have enjoyed sailing or going out on a fishing boat. In both of these types of boats, the windy waves will move your boat quite a bit. If you are in a fishing boat and you pick a spot that you want to "fish for a while," you need to put your anchor down or you will find yourself slowly drifting to a different part of the lake. Trust me, I've tried.

My cousin, Evan, is a top-notch fisherman who gets out on the water every time he can. He fishes 12 months out of the year because he lives on the riverbank in eastern Minnesota. He knows right where to put down his anchor for an extended time of fishing in one place. If I'm in a boat with him, I know that he will use the anchor to control our situation, and I know that our time will be safe and secure.

In our life with Christ, He keeps us safe and secure in all things. He is the protector of our heart and mind, the very anchor of the soul! Hebrews 6:19a states, "We have this hope as an anchor for the soul, firm and secure."

The NASB[1] puts it slightly differently, "This hope we have as an anchor of the soul, a hope both sure and steadfast..."

Both translations are solid, but as I studied the Greek word *psuches* (which is translated as the word "soul" in this verse), I realized that *psuches* means more than just your soul; it means your whole life. God will protect your whole life! Every area of your life! Commentator Frank Gaebelein agrees, "The author [of Hebrews] is not saying simply that hope secures the 'spiritual' [soul] aspect of man. He is affirming that hope forms an anchor for our whole life."[2]

We need to have this strong hope every day as we go through life! Our hope in Christ is our anchor! So put your anchor down deep into Christ.

Three words stuck out to me as I studied this verse, and they are easy to remember because they all start with the letter "S." We can picture these as the **three hooks** of our anchor of hope. And now I am picturing Evan pulling up an anchor and the three hooks are carrying seaweed from the bottom of the lake! *Classic times!*

Our hope in Christ is...

1. Sure

Heb. 6:19a (NASB) states, *"This hope we have as an anchor of the soul, a hope both sure..."*

2. Steadfast

"...and steadfast." (6:19, NASB)

3. Secure

Heb 6:19a (NIV) declares, *"We have this hope as an anchor for the soul, firm and secure."*

Walk confidently today because you have your hope in Christ as your anchor!

---

1. *New American Standard Bible*. La Habra, CA: Foundation Publications, for the Lockman Foundation, 1995. Print.

2. Gaebelein, Frank. *The Expositor's Bible Commentary*. Grand Rapids: Zondervan, 1981.

Joyful Noise

41

It was the first Sunday after Labor Day weekend during the fall of 2006. I was on campus in the city of La Crosse (WI) in the first semester of my senior year. One of my friends, whose name was John, invited me to join the gospel choir which practiced each Sunday night in the building right across from my apartment. My roommates and I had strategically chosen an apartment right across the street from campus and it paid off!

I came into that first choir practice with no expectations. I just looked for John, and he was in the tenor section and he "waved me over" to sit by him. I felt right at home, and I gelled with the group right way.

We performed concerts during both semesters and we even sang at a few E-Free churches as part of their Sunday morning worship services. I remember our Sunday at Bethany E-Free in La Crosse fondly, and I also remember our worship set at First Free in Onalaska, WI.

The memories are priceless, and we even had shirts that were made for our choir for the 2006-07 school year. The front of the shirt said *UWL Gospel Choir* and on the back it said **Make a Joyful Noise**. [UWL stands for University of Wisconsin-La Crosse.]

We wore these shirts proudly when we sang as a group and I would even wear my shirt on other days because I was proud to be in the choir.

One concert that stands out to me as special is our final concert at the end of the spring semester. It was the first weekend of May and my parents came down to visit me on campus. They wanted to see me perform with the choir, and they even took my friends John and Adam out to eat at Olive Garden!

John had a solo in one of our songs, and he belted it out with his excellent singing voice. The name of the song was called "We Lift Our Hands In The Sanctuary" and it comes from Psalm 134.

Psalm 134 is the last of 15 psalms that are called the *Psalms of Ascent*. Jewish pilgrims would come back to Jerusalem for special worship times on three separate occasions per year. They would **ascend** to Jerusalem. These psalms would commemorate their travel to and from Jerusalem and their time in the holy city.

<u>Ps 134</u> *Praise the Lord, all you servants of the Lord who minister by night in the house of the Lord. Lift up your hands in the sanctuary and praise the Lord. May the Lord bless you from Zion, He who is the Maker of heaven and earth.*

I was reading Matthew Henry's commentary on this psalm today, and he explained that the Levite priests were the servants of the Lord in the temple. Other pious Jews would help them attend to the temple activities and they would keep watch at night to protect from any intruders who may come to damage the sanctuary.[1] Henry writes, "[The helpers] must keep themselves awake and how can we spend our time better than praising God?"[2]

Henry continues, "It is a call to us to do it who, as Christians, are made priests to our God."[3]

We should **bless the Lord** at all times. We should long to linger in His presence with our fellow believers in the sanctuary. He is the Maker of heaven and earth. It is a privilege to praise Him.

The psalm gives us two *verbs* that we should do and then it gives a *benediction* to the worshipers.

It says we should **praise the Lord** and that we should **lift up our hands** in the sanctuary.

It is a wonderful thing to *lift our voices* and *our hearts* before Him in praise. We magnify Him and lift His Name high.

Let's receive this blessing from the Lord as the end-cap to this reading today. And let's remember that we are to be steady worshipers of the Lord as we make our pilgrimage through this life.

May the Lord bless you from Zion, He who is the Maker of heaven and earth.

---

1. Henry, Matthew. *Matthew Henry Commentary on the Whole Bible (Complete)*. 1706.

2. Ibid.

3. Ibid.

Youthful at Retirement

42

I have some friends who live in Arizona, and they are retired. **But I must say... they are incredibly youthful.** They live their life with an exuberance that is contagious and they trust God through the twists and turns of life.

Dave and Judy's recent road trip provided many twists and turns (literally) because they were driving through the Great West of the United States. Between Colorado, Idaho, Montana and California, they soaked in all that summer had to offer. They finished their *road odyssey* by driving down the west coast, and then they arrived back to their home-haven in Scottsdale, AZ.

Dave and Judy live life the way it was meant to be lived. They love their two sons, they appreciate their friends from around the country, and they enjoy God's playground (His creation) as they travel about the U.S.A. They provide a wonderful example for older people (and younger people) who want to make sure that they are living with energy and enthusiasm.

So, what is it that makes Dave and Judy so effective at living "on purpose"? In a word, *wisdom*.

Dave and Judy have a fresh wisdom that is consistently lived out day after day. It's not an old-timey wisdom that makes you think of an 85 year-old man with a cane and a few quips. No, it's an *active wisdom* that applies God's truth to everyday life.

The Book of James comes to mind when I think about a "wisdom book" in the New Testament. Dave and Judy live out the principles that are laid out in this insightful book. I encourage you to allow the nuggets of wisdom that the they employ to give you a boost. I believe that these golden nuggets from James will provide you with a roadmap to live with more *active wisdom* than you have in the past.

1. Ask God for wisdom.

If any of you lacks wisdom, you should ask God, who gives generously to all without finding fault, and it will be given to you. (James 1:5)

Dave and Judy are savvy and they are not slothful. God has blessed them with active wisdom and they have put it to use; they have made a difference in others' lives.

2. Get out and do God's work.

Do not merely listen to the word, and so deceive yourselves. Do what it says. (James 1:22)

Judy and Dave find many ways to serve, and they are regularly making (and maintaining) connections with others in order to speak into their lives.

3. Work steadily and don't compare yourself to others.

Let them show it by their good life, by deeds done in the humility that comes from wisdom. But if you harbor bitter envy and selfish ambition in your hearts, do not boast about it or deny the truth. (James 3:13b-14)

Dave and Judy avoid the "comparison trap," and they simply do what they believe God is calling them to do. They enjoy His many blessings as they go through the seasons of life.

4. Be supportive of others and cheer them on!

But the wisdom that comes from heaven is first of all pure; then peace-loving, considerate, submissive, full of mercy and good fruit, impartial and sincere. (James 3:17)

I recall many soccer games that I officiated in which Dave and Judy were on the sidelines cheering on one of the daughters of a family that they were friends with. In addition, they have provided encouragement for me. When I met them, I was dating Gracie and I had a lot of growing up to do. I can attest that I grew personally because of their ministry and other families at Cornerstone Community Church in Marshfield, WI.

Jesus is the true embodiment of wisdom. He is the way, the truth, and the life. He is the incarnate Son of God who sustains all things in the universe! We look to Him not only for wisdom, we look to Him for all things. Supremely, we look to Him for salvation. He gave Himself for us so that we would be saved from sin and walk in His ways.

I pray that you will cling to Jesus and lean on Him to guide you in the way of wisdom. Thankfully, the Lord provides us with many examples of Christian people who are walking out God's wisdom and sharing the gospel as they do it. Dave and Judy are just one example.

Who is an example of "active wisdom" in your life?

Perhaps you'll feel compelled to call them and thank them this week. Maybe you'll even soak in some more *fresh wisdom* when you chat with them. And remember, the wisdom and encouragement track flows both ways! They can receive encouragement from you, too!

You might even crack open the Book of James this week and discover some more wisdom nuggets that God wants to download into your soul.

Let's let the words of James conclude this installment. *If any of you lacks wisdom, you should ask God, who gives generously to all without finding fault, and it will be given to you.*

Bonus Section!

(3 Devotional Readings)

Wild and Free

43

Playing disc golf is a recreational activity that many people in the Midwest enjoy. I like the competitive aspect and the outdoor setting, so disc golf has become a favorite pastime of mine. I even set up a 9-hole disc golf course in my backyard and my neighbors' yards (with their permission).

The fond memories that I have of playing disc golf date back to my time living in Marshfield, WI. There was a nice 9-hole course near my house. I would jump on my bicycle (with disc in hand) and enjoy a couple of rounds at the *Wildwood Course* and then bike home. It was great!

The most challenging course, however, was on the other side of town. The *Braem Park Course* had many trees and creeks. It was not only a great 18-hole course, it was a celebration of nature! I remember playing countless rounds there with my friends, Paul and Jack, in the fall of 2008. All of us had unique schedules for our jobs, so we would often have free time in the middle of the day and we would go play some disc golf!

It was a competitive time, but it was also a time of great camaraderie. We enjoyed the challenge of trying to play our best round, and it was fun to be outdoors with friends. The weather was beginning to cool down, but we just kept playing! We didn't care! We just made sure to dress for the weather and we kept moving! We were the only ones on the course because nobody else wanted to play when it was that cold! We were ***wild and free***!

The reason that I can live free is that I know that I am loved by God. This allows me to rest in His grace and breath deep with His peace. I can enjoy His creation and live life the way it was meant to be lived.

In my Bible reading in 2 Thessalonians today, there was a verse at the end of chapter 2 that clearly summarized the ***many truths*** that enable us to have confidence and hope.

2 Thessalonians, 2:16-17 says, "*May our Lord Jesus Christ himself and God our Father, who loved us and by his grace gave us eternal encouragement and good hope, encourage your hearts and strengthen you in every good deed and word.*"

Let's look at four core truths that are evident in this passage. These four truths are life-changing if you allow them to be.

Truth #1: **We are loved by God.**

-> *"May our Lord Jesus Christ himself and God our Father, who loved us..."* (v. 16a)

Truth #2: **We have eternal encouragement through His grace.**

-> *"...and by his grace gave us eternal encouragement..."* (v. 16b)

Truth #3: **We have good hope through His grace.**

-> *"...and good hope..."* (v, 16c)

Truth #4: **God strengthens us in every good deed and word.**

-> *"...encourage your hearts and strengthen you in every good deed and word."* (v. 17)

A lot of people go through life and neglect to deeply contemplate these truths. We are loved by God! We have comfort and hope through His grace!

Why do we let other things distract us?

I think it is because we don't remind ourselves often enough of all the wonderful aspects of the gospel. During a recent Group Bible Study, one of the participants mentioned that we need to continually preach the gospel to one another. As Christians, we are leaky vessels and we need to have the pure water of the gospel poured on us regularly because we often forget the core truths that are foundational to our faith.

I trust that today's *short study* in 2 Thessalonians 2:16-17 was a helpful reminder that will encourage your heart as you take on another day.

You are loved by God. You have eternal encouragement through His grace. You have good hope by His grace. God strengthens you in every good deed and word.

Now, go live free and lift your eyes to the sky!

S.E.R.V.E.

44

I did some studying in the Word recently about the topic of serving, and I was able to dig up five helpful nuggets. I am glad to be able to share them with you here. Read on!

1. When you serve one another, you are **showing love** to others.

Galatians 5:13-14 says, "You, my brothers and sisters, were called to be free. But do not use your freedom to indulge the flesh; rather, serve one another humbly in love. For the entire law is fulfilled in keeping this one command: 'Love your neighbor as yourself.'"

2. When you serve, you are being an **example** to others.

2 Thessalonians 3:7-9 says, "For you yourselves know how you ought to follow our example. We were not idle when we were with you, nor did we eat anyone's food without paying for it. On the contrary, we worked night and day, laboring and toiling so that we would not be a burden to any of you. We did this, not because we do not have the right to such help, but in order to offer ourselves as a model for you to imitate."

3. When you serve one another, you are **refreshing others** by using your gift(s) to glorify God.

1 Peter 4:10 says, "Each of you should use whatever gift you have received to serve others, as faithful stewards of God's grace in its various forms."

4. When you work, you are doing what God created you to do. (Gen. 2:15)

Genesis 2:15 says, "The Lord God took the man and put him in the Garden of Eden to work it and take care of it."

Note: We need to live lives of **voluntary** service.

5. When you serve sacrificially, you are **exemplifying Christ.**

In Mark 10:45, Jesus says, "For even the Son of Man came not to be served, but to serve, and to give his life as a ransom for many."

Before Jesus went to the Cross, He began to show the disciples the high importance of sacrificial service, love, and equality through washing their feet.

John 13:14-15 says, "Now that I, your Lord and Teacher, have washed your feet, you also should wash one another's feet. I have set you an example that you should do as I have done for you."

In reference to Jesus washing his disciples' feet, Charles Ryrie states, "This dramatic scene of the foot-washing is a lesson in humility and a vivid portrayal of Christ's [humility]. Normally a servant performed this lowly task, further highlighting Christ's coming to serve."[1]

As I looked at the five points (above), and I looked at the word 'serve,' I realized that a helpful acrostic had just been naturally formed. Each part of the acrostric came from the 5 passages that I was studying. Hopefully, this will help you remember to SERVE.

Show love

Example

Refresh others

Voluntary

Exemplify Christ

Here are two take-away thoughts...

1. We are blessed to be a blessing.

2. Serving helps us grow to be more like Christ.

Here are three questions for you as you go.

How are you going to serve today?

How are you going to serve this week?

How are you going to serve this month?

———

1. Ryrie, Charles C. *Ryrie Study Bible: New American Standard Bible, 1995 Update*. Chicago: Moody Press, 1995. Print.

Teen Talk

45

I met with my church's youth group at the mall on a Sunday evening during the holiday season. You could tell that Christmas was in the air with all the Christmas trees and holiday decorations.

We split up into two groups to do the *escape rooms* at **Epoch Escapes**. Both of our groups were able to escape out of our respective rooms. The name of the two rooms were "Kraken Kwest" and "Outbreak 2020." Each group had to complete the challenge and escape their room in under 60 minutes. The Kraken team got out in 34 minutes and 46 seconds. The Outbreak team escaped in 44 minutes and 12 seconds. *Not bad at all! Quite impressive!*

The devotional time was rich and I was glad to be able to share with the students. The topic of my "Teen Talk" was quite important, so I titled my message *HUGE*.

As I began my message with the youth, I told them about a young man that I met at the YMCA recently. The guy's name was *Salvador*. The name Salvador (in Spanish) means Savior (in English). I said that we are going to talk about the great things that the Savior did for us. The awesome things that our Savior did for us are not small things; they are huge!

Jesus sustains the entire universe and He is glorious. He is over and above everything. I wanted my message to focus on the Cross and I wanted it to build from there. I chose to focus on three marvelous things that He did for us so I broke my message up into three parts.

The three parts were: 1) His crucifixion, 2) His resurrection, and 3) He gives us the Spirit. My theme verse was John 3:16, which says, "For God so loved the world that He gave His only Son, that whoever believes in Him shall not perish but have eternal life."

1. His crucifixion

Jesus took all of our sin on the Cross. All of it! Our past sins, our present sins, and our future sins. He took the sins of the whole world. This is a huge payment and an extremely painful and heavy burden to bear. But He did it for you; He did it for me. Romans 5:8 says, "But God demonstrates His own love for us in this: While we were still sinners, Christ died for us." He died the death that you (and I) deserve. He did this because we have sinned against Him and we need a Savior. He died in our place as a substitute, bearing the punishment that we were due. We accept His free gift of salvation by grace through faith.

2. His resurrection

Jesus paid it all on the Cross, but the proof that God accepted Jesus' sacrifice is that Jesus rose from the dead. We have victory and eternal life because He died and rose. He defeated death. _Because of Jesus, we have victory over darkness, death, sin, and Satan_. It was massively important that Jesus rose from the dead. 1 Corinthians 15:17 says, "And if Christ has not been raised, your faith is futile; you are still in your sins." In verse 20, Paul goes on to say, "But Christ has indeed been raised from the dead, the firstfruits of those who have fallen asleep." We have the victory because of Christ's resurrection. We can walk in Jesus' resurrection victory.

3. He gives us the Spirit

God gives us His Spirit. God is a giving God. He gave Jesus as a ransom on our behalf. Remember our theme verse. "For God so loved the world that He _gave_ His only Son." (emphasis added) After Jesus went to heaven, He sent the Holy Spirit to come and fill each believer. In Acts 1:8, Jesus instructs His disciples, "But you will receive power when the Holy Spirit comes on you; and you will be my witnesses in Jerusalem, and in all Judea and Samaria, and to the ends of the earth." The Holy Spirit being inside of us is a life-changing thing! God's Spirit gives us massive power to share the gospel, and we are given comfort through the Spirit.

God loves us so much and He wants to bless us. We are called to continually respond to the work of His Son and to cooperate with the work of His Spirit.

God wants to give comfort and strength to us as we move forward in life with Him. Look at our closing verse.

2 Chronicles 16:9a states, "For the eyes of the Lord range throughout the earth to strengthen those whose hearts are fully committed to him."

Let these gospel truths (and corresponding responses) refresh your soul as we wrap up today... God gives us a clean heart by grace through faith. We have been cleansed by the blood of the Lord Jesus Christ. The Lord rose again on the third day, and He will raise us on the last day to be with Him forever. God generously gives us His Spirit.

Offer praise to God for all that He's done for you. Specifically, thank the Lord Jesus for what He did for you at the Cross. Commit to living in obedience to the Holy Spirit, and _step forward in victory_.

Made in the USA
Monee, IL
13 June 2021